Master Painters of the
RENAISSANCE

Master Painters of the
RENAISSANCE

DAVID JACOBS

THE VIKING PRESS · NEW YORK

To my mother and father

ACKNOWLEDGMENTS

This book was talked out before it was written out. The many friends who
listened and answered back cannot be held responsible for my implications
and conclusions, but without their help I would not have been able to imply
anything or draw any conclusions about art in the first place. For their long-
time help I am especially indebted to my wife, and to Marc Porter, Richard
Ireland, and Mrs. Martha Shapp.

The author wishes to express his sincere thanks to the following collectors
and museums: National Gallery of Art, Washington, D.C., Detroit Institute
of Arts, Detroit, Michigan, Metropolitan Museum of Art, New York, New
York, Philadelphia Museum of Art, Philadelphia, Pennsylvania, The National
Gallery, London, Gemaldegalerie, State Museum, Berlin, Kunsthistorisches
Museum, Vienna, Art Color Slides, Inc., Art Reference Bureau, Camera Clix,
Inc.

D. J.

759 1. Paintings—History
2. Italian Renaissance
3. Art

CONTENTS

HUNT

LIST OF ILLUSTRATIONS

Author's Note

Giorgio Vasari (1511–74) was the voice of the Italian Renaissance. A good painter and architect, Vasari published a book in 1550 called *The Lives of the Eminent Architects, Painters, and Sculptors of Italy*. So important was this book that it totally overshadowed its author's painting and architecture, and it has taken a far greater place in history.

Commonly known by the simplified title *Lives of the Artists,* Vasari's book is not always reliable. When he could not find out what actually had happened, Vasari simply invented his "facts." But *Lives of the Artists* provides us with our earliest information about Renaissance masters. Ever since it was published, it has been the standard reference book from which all historians work.

More than his facts, it is Vasari's approach to art that has affected art history. *Lives of the Artists* regards the artist and his work as inseparable; the artist is given credit for his success and held responsible for his failure. This attitude was quite a departure from that of the Middle Ages, which had ended only a century before. In medieval times most masterpieces of art were created by anonymous craftsmen; but in the Renaissance, great artists became famous—in many cases, national heroes. And in the centuries since, the history of art has continued to be a story of individual achievement.

Our approach, like that of Vasari, will be to discuss the contributions of each individual artist. The ten Renaissance artists that are included have been chosen not necessarily because they were the ten greatest of the age, but because their achievements were widely varied. *Renaissance* is just a word that describes a length of time and a very special attitude. The most important thing to be learned from a discussion of the Renaissance is the fact that everyone who took part in it expressed something uniquely his own. It was a harmonious whole made of very different parts.

Master Painters of the
RENAISSANCE

WHAT WAS
THE RENAISSANCE?

The Renaissance was an age when man took a close look at himself and liked what he saw. Realizing that he had the ability to improve his mind and his world, he began to study the arts and sciences. Improving himself became his highest goal.

To Renaissance man, his was the best of all possible worlds, and he felt responsible for making it even better. Optimism, the chief attitude of the Renaissance, was reflected in the art of the age. Almost always the subject matter of art was man —man the powerful, man the thoughtful, man the glorious, man the greatest of God's creations.

Renaissance means rebirth. Unlike many periods in history, the Renaissance was given its name by the very people who participated in it. What was it that was being reborn? What was it that had died in the first place? And why did Renaissance man want to give it a new life? To answer these questions, we must look back, just as Renaissance man did, to the Classical Age of ancient Greece and Rome.

From the fourth century B.C. until the fourth century A.D., the Greeks and their successors, the Romans, ruled much of the Western world. In their way of life and in their art they were thoughtfully concerned with the workings of men's minds and the sources of life.

Classical Greek and Roman sculpture described the ideal human body. If we were to judge only from statues, we would think that the Greeks and Romans were strong, young, perfectly built men and women. Of course, they weren't, but these ancient peoples were not interested in showing the way ordinary people looked; instead they wanted to show man as he could look. This attempt at depicting ideal forms—according to certain standards—is what is meant by *classicism*.

Early in the fourth century A.D. the emperor Constantine made Christianity an official religion of the Roman Empire. Several years later, in 330, he moved his capital from Rome to the site of the ancient city of Byzantium, which he renamed Constantinople (now Istanbul, Turkey). Constantine's Eastern Christian, or Byzantine, Empire became the world's most powerful; while in the West, the Roman Empire soon fell to barbarian invaders. The barbarians enthusiastically accepted and spread Christianity. By the tenth century the formerly barbarian lands of Western Europe had united under the Church into a new Holy

14

Roman Empire that regained much of the lost power of ancient Rome.

The period roughly between 400 and 1300—during which Christianity became the Western world's main religion—has been named the Middle Ages. It was "in the middle" between the ancient world, which ended with the barbarian victory in Rome, and the Renaissance, the beginning of modern times.

During the Middle Ages, art was dominated by religious subject matter. The attitude of artists was quite different from what it had been in the Classical Age. Art no longer praised the virtue and beauty of man. Instead it served to remind him that he was but a tiny creation of God. Painting and sculpture became flat, unnatural looking, and very much alike. Architecture gradually changed from the simple to the monumental and complicated.

For the most part, medieval art in both the Roman and Byzantine Christian Empires was impersonal. Artists were not highly regarded. In fact, they apparently did not consider themselves to be very important, for they almost never signed their works. But in the twelfth and thirteenth centuries they became curious about life and art in the Classical Age. Some artists began to copy the well-proportioned carvings on Roman coins.

It was natural that the new interest in classical times should begin in Italy, for the Italians were surrounded with the remains of the ancient Roman era. The old Roman temples and public buildings were there for all to see. In time people discovered that they preferred the simplicity and less over-whelming proportions of these buildings to the huge, monu- 15 mental churches of the Gothic and Byzantine ages. In a medieval church men felt small and humble; in a Roman building they felt larger and more important.

In the libraries of Italian monasteries and universities, ancient books in Greek and Latin were reread. Scholars found that during the Classical Age the individual man and his achievements had been stressed. Medieval Christianity had, by and large, emphasized that life on earth was less important than life after death; but as the Middle Ages drew to a close, men worried more about life on earth. Scholars wanted to combine the logic of classicism with the beliefs of Christianity. Religious leaders, too, began to concern themselves with the intelligence as well as the spirit of the individual. One, an Italian monk called St. Thomas Aquinas (1225–74), wanted Christianity to be as acceptable to the educated man as it was to the peasant. A student of Greek philosophy, Aquinas used the reasoning of Aristotle to explain the ideas of his religion.

As the thirteenth century drew to a close the spirit of classical times filled the air. Poets and scholars urged others to look back to Greece and Rome for help in the making of a new, golden age of man. *Humanism,* an attitude in which the individual qualities of man are stressed, took hold. People looked at the stars and wondered about them; they looked across seas and wanted to know what was there; they looked at themselves and wondered how their minds and bodies worked. Most important, they began to look for their own answers. Though recalling the past for help, they were really concerned with the future—and they envisioned a future on earth as well as one in heaven.

16

The men of the Renaissance were harsh judges of the Middle Ages—perhaps too harsh. Nevertheless, they thought that man had been in the dark for too long, and they did something about it. Tired of night, they longed for day. They read, they talked, they experimented, and whether they were right or wrong about the Middle Ages, they did create a golden age that continues to inspire and influence men to this day.

THE DAWN
OF THE RENAISSANCE

Giotto

The Middle Ages were ending. In the nighttime darkness there were fresh breezes that filled the Italian air with new spirit. Then dawn broke over the cities of Siena and Florence, and painters prepared for day.

Dawn belongs as much to night as to day, for it ends the darkness and begins the light. The last quarter of the thirteenth century and the first quarter of the fourteenth belonged to both the Middle Ages and the Renaissance. The great painters of the time prepared for the new age by summing up the old. Four artists who helped build the bridge between medieval and Renaissance painting were Cimabue, Duccio, Giotto, and Simone Martini.

18   Cimabue (1240?–1302?) (see page 43) is the least famous

of the four. Very little is known about his life, and we cannot even be certain that all the paintings said to be his really are his. To be sure, artists in the thirteenth century were already being recognized for their individual skills. But they had not yet achieved the hero's position that later Renaissance artists would enjoy, and historians of their own time seldom wrote their biographies. It was still the man's work and not the man himself that was applauded.

Duccio di Buoninsegna (1255?–1319) (see page 42) and Cimabue were still deep in the tradition of Byzantine painting. They used flat, geometric backgrounds richly decorated with gold. But both took giant steps toward making more natural-looking figures. The bodies they painted were somewhat shaded to look round and solid, and the faces expressed human feelings.

If a spirit of independence was in the air, then it must have been Duccio who breathed most deeply. Though his art was still an echo of the past, there was nothing medieval in his behavior. Discipline, obedience, faith, patriotism, and humility—all fine traits rigidly enforced in the Middle Ages— played little part in the life of Duccio. He was continuously hauled into court and fined. We can't be sure what all his offenses were, but they included political crimes, refusal to serve in the army, refusal to pay debts and taxes, and practicing sorcery. Despite his frequent quarrels with Church officials, he received many contracts from them and painted altarpieces for churches in Siena and elsewhere.

Characteristic of the Renaissance was the interest that men had in their world. Expressive of this were Giotto (1276?– 1337) and Simone Martini (1284–1344). Like Cimabue and

Duccio, the younger artists were filled with the spirit of humanism. But they took another forward step. To describe the close relationship between man and nature, they painted pictures that told stories, placing their characters in natural settings. The flat, patterned backgrounds of medieval art were put aside, and for the first time since the days of Greece and Rome, man was shown at his greatest— as master of his own world.

The most famous painting by Simone Martini is the *Annunciation* (see page 42), painted in *tempera* (a kind of paint made with color, egg yolks, and water) and gold on a wooden panel. Because the angel Gabriel is a heavenly messenger, he wears a cloudy-white robe ornamented with gold and a wind-blown cloak of blue and gold. The Virgin's chair is covered with orange and gold brocade. The Latin words of the angel's greeting are raised on the gold background. Although the angel and the Virgin could be anywhere, the gold and color show that these are royal, heavenly persons.

But it was Giotto who broke most completely from the medieval tradition. In his paintings he used less detail than Simone did, and he placed his characters in familiar settings and in everyday clothing. Only the halos above their heads suggested that these people were different from ordinary men and women.

From Giotto onward, the history of art is a story of men. Each lived in his own time, and the work of each reflects that time; but more important, each speaks for himself. The genius of the artist's mind—not just the marks of his brush

—is what we see in his art.

Giotto

Genius alone did not make Giotto the father of all Renaissance painters. Like most of history's heroes, he lived at the right time in the right place, and fate contributed to his development. Born around 1276, Ambrogiotto di Bondone grew up in a quickly but quietly changing Italy. That his father was a peasant but was not poor is indicative of the changing times: prosperity would hardly have been possible for a herder of sheep and goats a century earlier.

The Bondone family lived in the hills, a few miles north of Florence. Close enough to benefit from the artistic progress taking place in that great city, the young Giotto was at the same time far enough away to avoid involvement in the civil wars being fought by Florentines. His was a peaceful boyhood, free from poverty and struggle.

Little is known of his youth; much of what we do know is based on hearsay. It is said that Giotto's father was an affectionate man, devoted to his son. When Giotto was eight or nine, Bondone gave him a few sheep to watch. Herding can be a lonely job, but Giotto loved to tend the sheep and watch them graze as he sat in the shade. If he found a sheet of slate, he would draw a picture of the animals on it with a pointed rock. Gradually, the crude childlike drawings grew more complex, and Giotto tried to show the way the animals' bodies were made. His artist's eye noted the way the sheep moved, and he learned to select only the most important lines to show this movement. Finally, he began to add a peasant or two to his drawings.

Unaware of the revolutionary thing he was doing, the young Giotto thus brought to art the custom of drawing from nature. Landscape painting was not formally developed for several centuries, and artists did not start to paint out-of-doors until the 1880s; yet the later landscapists all sprang from Giotto, the first to express in his work the interrelationship of man and his surroundings.

In *Lives of the Artists,* Vasari wrote of the first meeting of Cimabue and Giotto. We know the two did meet, because we can now be sure that Giotto became the pupil of Cimabue. But this meeting may not have been so charming as the writer suggested it was. Still, since no other account can be found, we might at least give Vasari the courtesy of repeating his story.

Vasari tells us that one day the affairs of Cimabue took him from Florence to Vespignano, the little village where Giotto lived. On his journey Cimabue came upon the young artist sitting by the roadside. As his sheep grazed around him, Giotto was busily drawing pictures of them. The Florentine halted, astonished at the untrained boy's ability. When Cimabue asked Giotto if he would like to study in his home in the city, the youngster said yes, but that the decision was up to his father. Cimabue asked Bondone, who agreed.

And so, Giotto left home to study in Cimabue's workshop. Cimabue must have been a marvelous teacher, instructing Giotto in every aspect of the artist's craft. The young artist worked from dawn until dark every day—including holidays. He learned the *fresco* method of painting, in which water-color paints are applied to damp plaster; and the more complicated tempera technique. Oil paint had not yet been

22

developed. The artist had to work with great care, making
decisions in seconds, for fresco and tempera dry almost in-
stantly. Changes are difficult and sometimes impossible to
make. Giotto mastered both media while still a boy.

Giotto was in himself a tribute to his master. Despite the
rigid training and strict discipline that Cimabue imposed,
Giotto always remained independent and original. His
work hardly resembles Cimabue's. Painting landscape backgrounds and scenes of everyday life was out of the question
for most men of Cimabue's generation. But Cimabue was too
wise to challenge Giotto's right to introduce new settings as
well as new techniques to art.

Giotto's ability to express affection for the commonplace
was his second great accomplishment. Religion still dominated art—as it would for years to come—but Giotto told
Bible stories in a visual language that anyone could understand. He never lost his love for the animals and peasants he
had grown up with, and they appear in his paintings time
and time again. They surround the saints who preach and
work their miracles by the riverside. He painted the Virgin
Mary to look like any peasant mother as she gazes lovingly
at the infant in her arms. No longer is she the lone figure of
medieval times, painted flatly against a background of wood
and gold; instead she is a human mother to whom simple
viewers could feel close and familiar. The newborn Christ
sucks his thumb.

Word of Giotto's great skill spread. We are not certain
when he left the workshop of Cimabue, but after he did he
was called to Assisi to decorate the upper church. On these
walls Giotto painted scenes from the life of St. Francis (see

page 45). What so startled the church leaders was the fact that Giotto depicted the saints as men of his own time, dressed in clothing that any Italian peasant of the thirteenth century might have worn. Thus the common man realized that the saints of history were flesh-and-blood men, like himself. To give even more life to his paintings, the young master chose the most important moment in each story to illustrate. The characters seem to move reasonably, even though Giotto knew very little about how the body actually works. And, despite the fact that the science of perspective was unfamiliar to him, Giotto managed to make the figures appear to exist in real space.

Giotto was an intelligent, independent person. His friends included some of the greatest figures of his age; best known is Dante, author of *The Divine Comedy*. Evidence suggests that the artist was even-tempered and had a fine sense of humor. After Giotto had completed the frescoes at Assisi, Pope Boniface VIII sent a representative to see him. The Pope wanted frescoes painted in St. Peter's Church in Rome, and his agent asked Giotto to submit some sort of illustration as a sample from which the Pope could make a decision. Giotto probably felt that the Pope's request was a bit insulting. After all, the Assisi paintings were available to anyone who wanted to see his work. Feeling that his reputation had already been firmly enough established, the master resented being asked to submit a sample. Not one to lose his temper, he replied with a grand gesture. While the representative stood by, Giotto tacked a piece of vellum to the wall, picked up a brush, and in one sweeping motion painted a nearly perfect circle. It was not a gesture intended to shock or impress; any competent artist of the age could have done the same. Instead it was a statement half-jokingly intended to assert his independence. He would work if the project were given to him, but he would not work to get the job. The Pope's reaction is unknown, but in any case the commission did go to Giotto.

By 1300 Giotto was the most famous painter in Italy. He was soon called to the town of Padua to paint the walls of the Arena Chapel. Here his humanism can best be seen. In *Flight into Egypt* (see page 41)—one of his many wall pictures of the Virgin, of Christ, the Crucifixion, and the Day of Judgment—Mary wraps her child in a cloak to protect him. The journey is dangerous, and she clasps the baby tightly. Ahead, leading the donkey, Joseph turns and looks back, as any husband would. Among the citizens of Padua, even the illiterate must have felt what the people in the painted scene felt: danger, anxiety, love.

A fine sculptor and architect as well as a painter, Giotto was appointed director of architecture of Florence in 1334. There he designed the famous bell tower, now known as Giotto's Tower, for the Cathedral of Florence, but he died in 1337 before it had been completed.

After Giotto's death his fame lasted, and masters of the Renaissance looked to his work for inspiration and influence. Few artists in history have been so widely respected by those who followed them. Being called "Father" by so many is a tremendous responsibility—one that the genius of Giotto has borne well through the ages.

FLORENCE:
FLOWER OF THE
RENAISSANCE

Masaccio

Piero della Francesca

Botticelli

Giotto had many students and followers, none of whom were talented enough to enlarge upon what the master had brought to painting. Thinking that they could continue the march toward realism, they were much less inventive than the shepherd had been. Indeed, a painting or two might have contained figures more accurately drawn than those in Giotto's work, but the increased naturalism was achieved at the expense of human understanding or quality of design.

Things did not soon improve. Simone Martini—not a Renaissance painter, though an important one just the same —died in Siena seven years after Giotto. For one of the last times in history, painting lacked a working genius. More-26 over, the terrible epidemic known as the Black Death raged through Europe. In 1348, three-fifths of the population of Florence died from the plague. The aristocrats and merchants, still jealous of one another, still anxious to rule the commerce of Florence in this era of active international trade, might have helped one another and the community to recover from the devastation. Instead they battled harder than ever. When their fighting combined with the effects of the plague, the social structure of Florence collapsed; but although class distinctions were wiped out, Florentines did not feel brotherly. While people fell dead on the streets, the survivors struggled to form a new upper class. Those that succeeded hated each other, and local wars between them contributed to the chaos of life. This was hardly what could be called an atmosphere for a "rebirth."

Finally, the struggle for power produced a winner. The Medici family took control of Florentine government in 1427 and ruled for more than a century. As leaders they weren't perfect, but they may well have contributed more to the progress of an age than any ruling family of any time. Such modern-day systems as the graduated income tax were employed to finance the Medici government. From the family fortune, acquired mostly through international banking, they established worthwhile charities and patronized the arts. As a result, the foundling hospital built by the family has both social and artistic importance in history. Established to house the orphaned and neglected children of Florence, it was representative of the civic improvements made during the Medici rule. And the building itself, designed by Filippo Brunelleschi (1377–1446), is one of the most important in the history of architecture. The first Renaissance building in Florence, it was revolutionary in design and function. 27

Throughout the ten centuries that preceded the Renaissance, monumental architecture had been reserved for great churches and castles. But the Hospital of Innocents was built for the poor and homeless. That the orphans of Florence lived in the greatest building of the time symbolizes that humanism had really taken hold.

The Church had long been the chief patron of the arts. Now the Medici became a leading customer. Not only did they commission work, but they also felt responsible for locating talent and making certain that proper training was available. In the garden of his palace, Lorenzo de Medici established what was probably the first modern art school. There painters and sculptors, including such masters as Botticelli and Michelangelo, met each other, studied, talked, argued, ate, and even slept if they wanted to. There the greatest scholars of the time congregated, and the artists could not help but participate in discussions about poetry, philosophy, and science. As they learned their craft, artists became intellectuals, competent in dealing with the ideas of politics, literature, religion, or mathematics.

Under the Medici the Renaissance flowered. How fitting it seems that the golden sun of a great age should have shone first on Florence! (The Italian name of the city, *Firenze,* means flower.) Ideas were exchanged, results of scientific experiments were shared, investigations were made together. The men who were most admired were those who had many interests. Thus, artists were frequently more than just painters, sculptors, or architects: many were all three. Moreover, Leonardo was an inventor, Fra Angelico a monk, Piero della Francesca a mathematician, Michelangelo a poet,

28

and Vasari a historian-author. Not all were Florentines by birth, but their hunger for knowledge and ideas was fed by products grown in the Medici garden.

Humanism had been introduced into Italian painting by Giotto. Around the time when the Medici were emerging as the first family of Florence, this spirit had already become part of the young tradition of Renaissance art. But new breezes blew, carrying the excitement of scientific discovery. Where Giotto had succeeded in giving his subjects human qualities, painters now wanted to add something else: accuracy.

In order to learn how to show the exact proportions of the human body and precisely how it works, fifteenth-century Florentine artists studied anatomy. Drawing from models and skeletons, they found out how the human body is put together. Hours were spent sketching hands, feet, necks, and other individual parts of the body. They learned which muscles tense and which relax when a man kneels. They learned how bones move when a woman walks up steps. They learned the difference between the skin on a baby's forehead, which is white and smooth, and on his thighs, which is fleshy and pink.

Although they were able to depict the body accurately, some painters found that their figures still looked flat and almost weightless. Slowly they began to realize that light and shadow are responsible for making an object look thick or thin, round or flat. The term *modeling* means reproducing the effects that light creates. We can't be sure when painters first learned to use the technique, but in fifteenth-century Florence it was widely employed. When modeling, 29 the painter first determines the direction from which the light comes. Whichever side of an object faces that direction appears brighter and lighter than the side not struck by light. Therefore, if a woman is to be painted outdoors in the late afternoon, the source of light is, of course, the sun, low in the western sky. If she is looking to the south, her right profile appears lighter than her left. Her nose and lower lip cast shadows, which vary the darkness of her left profile. And, by reproducing the shadow she casts on the grass, the artist shows that the girl is solid and occupies space.

While they learned anatomy and modeling, fifteenth-century Florentine painters also discovered the value of using *perspective* to make their scenes seem more natural. Just before the Medici emerged as rulers of Florence, Brunelleschi—later the architect of the foundling hospital—spent several years in Rome studying the ruins of the Classical Age. Fascinated that the Roman architects had been able to achieve the appearance of perfect balance with their ancient instruments, Brunelleschi measured the various parts of the buildings. He was amazed to find that some parts were much higher, longer, shorter, or wider than they looked. He concluded that there were ways of making the appearance of great depth—even on a flat or nearly flat surface. Single-handedly he worked out the mathematical rules for perspective. His main observation was that all parallel lines, if continued indefinitely, seem to meet at the horizon. If an artist wants to draw a building that appears to have depth as well as height and width, he must draw the structure as though the lines of the roof and ground would, if extended, come together where the ground seems to meet the sky. Therefore, the corner farthest from the viewer's eye must be painted smaller than the corner nearest to him. Everyone knows the often used but perfect example of perspective: a railroad track. If you stand in the middle, the rails will seem to come together at the horizon. It is amazing that our sight and mind work so well together: the eye sees in perspective so that we may judge distances; the brain tells us at the same time that our eye is lying, that the rails really don't meet at all.

Brunelleschi returned to Florence and taught his rules to others. Though bitter over his earlier loss of a design contest (for a pair of sculpted bronze doors in the Baptistery of Florence), Brunelleschi even taught perspective to the sculptor who had defeated him, Lorenzo Ghiberti (1378–1455). The Renaissance was just getting under way, but already the ideals must have been well established; for Brunelleschi's gesture certainly represented the spirit of the age. When universal greatness was a goal, knowledge was the property of everyone.

In view of the closeness of the artistic community of Florence, it is astonishing that the many painters who worked there were able to develop along widely varied lines. With remarkably little study, a viewer has no trouble distinguishing between their works. Many artists stressed the newly discovered scientific approach to painting. Some continued along the lines of Giotto, showing saints as peasants, bringing to art (and to religion) the qualities of peace and humility. Others described the heroic possibilities of man, representing religious figures as Greek gods and goddesses.

Fra Angelico (1400?–1455) concentrated on telling the spiritual side of Bible stories. Though the figures in his paintings may be in mourning, they are bathed in heavenly light, symbolizing the artist's religious faith and optimism. Fra Angelico's opposite was Fra Filippo Lippi (1406?–69). The model for his Virgin was clearly a local Florentine girl, and the saints who surround her look old, worn, and weary. Lippi was an early realist, representing life as he saw it—not judging it, not praising it, not employing symbols of faith. Yet, the fact that he pictured Joseph as a wrinkled old man indicates a kind of optimism. Like Giotto, he says to all men that the saints they admire and worship were, before all else, men like themselves.

Florence: Flower of the Renaissance

Among the greatest of Florentine painters were Masaccio (1401–28), Piero della Francesca (1420?–92), and Sandro Botticelli (1445?–1510). Each represents one of the dominant courses of fifteenth-century painting. To Masaccio, man was a hero because he could overcome the vices of the world. The figures in his paintings know shame and fear as well as pity and bravery. Piero was interested less in capturing the significance of an event than in depicting the orderly and timeless quality of his religious subjects. Botticelli liked to express his love of nature and devotion to religion by telling poetic tales on his canvas; indeed, he called his pictures "poems."

Masaccio was the first great painter after Giotto. In the splendid atmosphere of Florence, he lived for just a moment in history. But he picked up where Giotto had stopped and set Renaissance painting on its way.

Masaccio

In the paintings of Masaccio can be found grandeur, drama, realism, elegance, and honesty. He praised men, yet he painted them as they were. A humanist, he studied anatomy, modeling, and perspective. These techniques were new, and he devoted his whole career to their mastery. He also used light to bathe and highlight his religious figures. And for centuries after his death Italian artists studied his work.

Masaccio set painting on a path from which it would not stray for some 350 years. Like Giotto, Michelangelo, and the sculptor Donatello, he spent his life summing up what had been learned in the past while creating an approach for the future. But what makes Masaccio's accomplishment even greater is the fact that his career lasted only eight years, his life only twenty-seven.

Very little is known about that brief life. Tommaso di Ser Giovanni de Mone was born near Florence in 1401. Big, fumbling, awkward, he was nicknamed Masaccio, "Hulking (clumsy) Tom." According to Vasari, he studied with a painter named Masolino (1383?–1447?). Some scholars agree; others think that Masolino was the student of Masaccio, who, though younger, was the better painter. In either case, *The Virgin and Child with St. Anne* was painted around 1420 by both artists. This is Masaccio's earliest surviving work.

In 1422 Masaccio was enrolled in the Medici art school. 33

He continued to work with Masolino and did not produce anything on his own (as far as we know) until 1426—only two years before his death. This was an altarpiece painting. for the Carmelite Church at Pisa. Never before had the full style and all the elements of Renaissance painting been used. The altarpiece, which is now in very bad condition, contained pictures of the Virgin and Child, the Crucifixion, and several saints.

A year later, back in Florence, Masaccio was working on his masterpiece: the frescoes on the Brancacci Chapel walls in the Church of the Carmine. One series of paintings on the chapel walls illustrates the life of St. Peter. In the *Tribute Money* (see detail page 45) the tax collector has come to town. The people are poor, and St. Peter knows that they cannot pay. In the center of the picture Jesus tells Peter where he has to look to find the money. In another scene St. Peter walks down a street lined with cripples; his shadow is healing them. They do not rush to him or beg for help, but their faces express quiet faith.

In another panel in the chapel entitled *The Expulsion of Adam and Eve from Paradise* (see page 47), Masaccio has stripped the two figures in all respects: their feelings are as bare and exposed as their bodies. They have sinned, and they know it; Eve covers herself in shame, her agonized face looks heavenward. Adam hides his crying face in his hands. Witness to the despair is the angel sent to expel them, whose expression is mysterious. Perhaps the angel wonders whether the suffering of Adam and Eve is a good sign, a sign that man wants to be perfect, even though he sins.

34 In two years Masaccio established the course of later Ren-

aissance painting. His approach was scientific—he employed perspective and modeling to be as accurate as possible. The expressions of his figures were subtle and not always easily understood—just as the facial expressions of real people are often subtle. This impressed Leonardo, who wrote that Masaccio had clearly shown that nature was the mistress of all masters.

But Masaccio's approach was also heroic and human. Adam and Eve are not viewed as two different people, each suffering. Instead they function as a unit, suffering at once, perhaps expressing the despair of all mankind. Yet the ability of the first couple to suffer at once, to share each other's guilt, reminds us that man is really a heroic being, able to overcome, through love, his wrongdoing. This attitude, in which sin and heroism are subtly tied together, was later to influence Michelangelo, who often copied Masaccio's Brancacci Chapel pictures.

Masaccio's use of space was also new. The panel on which the *Expulsion* was painted is very narrow; yet the figures move quickly, as though their space were not limited. The picture turns into a window; if we, the viewer, were to arrive at the window a moment later, Adam and Eve would be gone, a hundred feet away perhaps. Thus we are made to understand that the panel itself shows only a small portion of what goes on in life. It is suggested that events take place to the right and left, above and below the picture edges. This attempt to capture movement at a given moment was later adopted and perfected by Raphael.

And, finally, Masaccio brought to painting a new concern with light. The face of Christ in the *Tribute Money* illuminates Him and draws our attention to Him. St. Peter, too, is highlighted, since he is the main subject of the panel. As he walks down the street lined with the sick, the architectural detail above his head is struck by sunlight, emphasizing the scene taking place below. No one knows whether the development of painting techniques would have been quickened had Masaccio lived a longer life. But the emphasis on the effects of light at which Masaccio hinted was not taken up by such masters as Titian until a century had passed.

The achievements of Masaccio have never been in doubt. Since his death in 1428 his work has never gone out of fashion and has seldom been seriously attacked by critics. We know almost nothing about his life; we have very few paintings from which we can study his career. All the same, he is a giant. His position in the history of art is based on nothing other than his work. That is his most gigantic accomplishment.

Piero della Francesca

Masaccio's life was short; but his influence lasted for generations and his reputation for centuries. In contrast, Piero della Francesca's life was long; his influence was rejected by his own students; and his work was neglected after the Renaissance. If his paintings were discussed at all, they were considered old-fashioned, cold and inhuman, closer in style to the Gothic Age than to the Renaissance. Piero seemingly had little to say: his art expressed nothing about the heroism of man, the glory of faith, or the beauty of nature.

36 In the second half of the nineteenth century, new life was

breathed into the art of Piero della Francesca. A number of English scholars, reacting against the decline of artistic craftsmanship during the Industrial Revolution, revived interest in the art of old. They were especially fond of medieval and early Renaissance art. Raphael and Titian had been among the most popular Renaissance painters; now Botticelli and Fra Filippo Lippi came into fashion. Less famous than the others, Piero was nevertheless brought into light on their coattails. But not until the genius of the modern French painter Paul Cézanne (1839–1906) began to influence the development of modern art did artists begin to acknowledge the full significance of Piero's work.

Piero della Francesca

Artists tend to view the history of art from the standpoint of their own work. Before our century painters favored artists of the past whose styles provided backgrounds for their own. After Cézanne's death and as the century progressed, his approach was enlarged upon and became a chief characteristic of modern art. Dividing the flat canvas in an orderly fashion was the new problem; subject matter and naturalism became less important. It was logical, therefore, that modern artists, trained in the tradition of Cézanne and cubism, should look with interest and respect to Piero, to whom structure was more important than subject, to whom mathematical perfection was more important than storytelling.

The mathematician-artist was born in Borgo San Sepolcro, a small town in central Italy, around 1420. When he was very young, he developed an extraordinary curiosity about a vast number of things. He studied mathematics, practiced drawing, and read Latin classics. At twenty he left Borgo and went to Florence to study with Domenico Veneziano (died 1461), a good teacher who immediately allowed Piero to assist him in painting important commissions. A worldly, well-spoken young man, Piero was introduced to many influential people, including the Duke and Duchess of Urbino, whose portraits he later painted (see page 46). He returned frequently to his home town and served several terms on the town council.

Piero applied his brilliant mathematical theories to his style of painting. Especially interested in geometry and perspective, he rendered the human figure as if it were a combination of geometrical shapes. Instead of working from live models all the time, he often made clay spheres, cylinders, cubes, and cones. He worked like an architect, constructing his paintings in a way that made every part appear to depend on others for support. Thus, the rectangle of the sky was supported as though it were a roof by rows of people serving as columns.

Piero's subject matter is seldom emphasized in the conventional sense. If he depicted a battle scene, his "message" was rarely war; he offered no judgment about the heroism or misery of man. If the details tell us that his pictures are full of action and events, our good eyes tell us otherwise; for no matter how eventful the topic, a Piero painting always appears solid and stately, geometric, immovable, and calm. Whatever message about the apparent subject we might expect is dimmed by the artist's emphasis on structure. His real message is that objects and events, whether made by nature or man, are based on the orderly scheme of the universe. Perhaps he felt that orderliness was God's work. This being 38 the case, his paintings are deeply religious. Though they may not illustrate the human devotion to the Almighty, his paintings display confidence in the patterns of life. No momentary feeling is expressed; instead, Piero went beyond the moment and tried to capture the essence of things. Pain and suffering last only for measurable time; order is eternal.

Piero is probably the hardest Renaissance painter to talk about. If you find this discussion of his work too difficult to understand, you are not unusual. But if you look at his paintings and study more and more about art, the message of Piero will gradually become clear. And as you do come to understand him, you will find it impossible to explain his work to anyone else. This is what makes Piero unique. His art is purely visual and belongs to the eye and mind. Translating his message into the language of words somehow seems to lose that very message.

When Piero was around fifty, he went to work for the Duke of Urbino, a wealthy art patron who frequently invited artists from all nations to his palace. There Piero met Justus van Ghent (active 1460–75), a Flemish painter. From Justus, with whom he worked for several years, Piero learned how to use oil paint, a new medium invented in Flanders early in the fifteenth century. By using this versatile medium, Piero was able to carry further his experiments with light. He had been interested in capturing the effects of atmospheric light for some time and was one of the first painters to employ the *chiaroscuro* technique, in which light and dark are sharply contrasted. Piero taught his students how to use oil paint, and how to work effectively with light; but thinking it old-fashioned, they rejected his geometrical style.

Techniques were much less important to Piero than structure, and as he grew older, the science of perspective and mathematics interested him more and more. By the 1470s his sight may have been failing (evidence suggests that he was blind when he died). Apparently he was anxious to spend more time working out his scientific theories, so he returned to Borgo and gave up painting for good. Until his death in 1492, he wrote books on mathematics, perspective, and painting.

Piero represented the peak of scientific Renaissance painting. In the sixteenth century, Renaissance art took another path—the one paved by naturalism. Piero's work, though still widely admired, gradually fell into neglect.

Botticelli

This is what we know of Botticelli: he was born in Florence, probably in 1445, seldom left the city, and died there in 1510.

His real name was Alessandro Filipepi, and he was the son of a leather tanner. His father's friends called Alessandro's older brother Botticello, which in Italian means little barrel, because of his shape. When the artist was born they referred to him as Botticelli (*celli* is smaller than *cello*).

In 1460 "the littlest barrel" was probably studying with Fra Filippo Lippi. By the time he was twenty-five, Botticelli had earned a reputation as one of the best painters in Florence and had already become the teacher of Lippi's son.

When he did depart from Florence, he usually went no farther than Rome. In 1481 Pope Sextus IV invited Botticelli to the Vatican to do a painting in the just-completed

Giotto. *Flight into Egypt.*

Scrovegni Chapel, Padua

Simone Martini. *Annunciation*.

Cimabue. *Crucifix.*   *San Domenico, Arezzo*

opposite: Duccio. *Calling of Apostles Peter and Andrew.*   *National Gallery, Washington, D. C.*

Fra Angelico and Fra Filippo Lippi. *Adoration of the Magi.*   *National Gallery, Washington, D. C.*

Giotto. *St. Francis Preaching to the Birds.*

Upper Church of San Francesco, Assisi

Masaccio. *The Tribute Money* (detail).

Santa Maria della Carmine, Florence

Botticelli. *Primavera.*

Piero della Francesca.
Duke of Urbino
and *Duchess of Urbir*

Uffizi Gallery, Florence

Masaccio. *Expulsion of Adam and Eve from Paradise.*

Santa Maria della Carmine, Florence

Botticelli. *Birth of Venus.*   *Uffizi Gallery, Florence*

Sistine Chapel. There he did a series of murals illustrating the life of Moses.

After his return to Florence, he may have lived at the Medici palace for a short time. Whether he did or not, Botticelli was influenced by the scholars who frequented the palace garden. He was very much interested in their studies of classical history and literature and was impressed with their efforts to unite the spirituality of Christianity with the logic of Greek philosophy. He became a student of the writings of the ancient Greek, Plato. In his art he gave his religious figures the heroic qualities of mythological gods and goddesses.

In later years Botticelli changed his attitude. The fanatic monk Savonarola, active in the 1490s, was convinced that Florentine life was utterly corrupt (which it may well have been). He preached for a return to the religious values of the Middle Ages and thought the classical influence inspired anti-religious thinking. The monk was extremely powerful for a while; after the Medici were driven from Florence in 1494 at Savonarola's own urging, he became dictator of the city-state. Four years later he went too far, urged the expulsion of the Pope, and antagonized even the monks of his order. He was executed in 1498.

While Savonarola lived Botticelli was probably indifferent to his fanaticism—at least no record indicates otherwise. But after the monk's death, Botticelli grew fascinated with his preachings. The artist became more religious and may even have destroyed some of his earlier non-religious works. Until his death he painted only Christian subjects and tried to eliminate signs of classical influence.

49

Even this much cannot be proved. Most of what we know about Botticelli has come through the ages by word of mouth. His paintings were not highly regarded immediately after his death and, like Piero's work, did not receive a great deal of attention until the nineteenth century. But Botticelli's pictures tell us much about the man. His view of the Renaissance was very personal. Of all the artists discussed in this book, Botticelli was the one most attracted to the ideas of the Classical Age. He loved Greek and Roman mythology, and even his religious paintings contain figures that resemble his depictions of gods and goddesses. Yet he was apparently always attracted to the decorative art of the Middle Ages. Whether his subjects came from religion, poetry, or mythology, his figures were elongated and stylized and his backgrounds richly patterned, much like the backgrounds in medieval art.

Botticelli was fascinated by the beginnings of things; birth meant innocence unmarked by the harshness of life. He did not paint a simple symbol of love; he pictured the birth of the love goddess (see page 48). He did more than capture the beauty of nature; he caught the moment of spring's bloom (see page 46). And he favored the birth of Christ over all other illustrations of Christianity.

During all periods certain attitudes affect all the arts. The humanism of the Renaissance is reflected in the literature of the age as well as the painting, the music as well as the drama. Usually, looking too hard for parallels among the arts is not a good idea; you find relationships that no artist ever intended.

In the case of Botticelli, however, making comparisons is

hard to avoid. His human figures are graceful and lyrical: they look like dancers. Every element works in harmony with all others. In the *Birth of Venus,* the gentle curve of the goddess of love's hip and leg is duplicated and enlarged on the shell that surrounds her. The same lines are repeated in the water, trees, and clouds, giving the painting a softly rhythmical quality. There is no better way to explain the relationships of the lines than to say that they rhyme. The master himself called his pictures poems, and others have called them songs. Indeed they are: they sing in praise of beauty.

Botticelli was for years unconcerned that Savonarola thought his work, and work like it, to be pagan and evil. Apparently, however, the manner in which the monk was executed (hanged, then burned) came as a great shock to the artist. He began to regard his own success as proof of the corrupt life he had lived. At first he tried to eliminate the "sinful" qualities in his pictures; then he stopped painting altogether. He probably retired to a monastery, spending the last decade of his life praying and repenting for creating some of the most delicately and lovingly executed pictures ever to soothe a weary viewer.

THREE GIANTS

Leonardo da Vinci

Raphael

Michelangelo

When one great genius is born, it is in the very nature of things that he shall not stand alone. In the same place, at the same time, others live, too, as though to stimulate each other by a rivalry of excellence.

VASARI

Leonardo da Vinci

Leonardo has a matchless reputation today. That he has any reputation at all seems almost a miracle. Time, luck, and the master himself seem to have done everything to prevent it.

Leonardo is known as a fine sculptor. Some casts have been made of his small models, but nothing was ever cast full-sized in bronze. For an important monument he modeled a life-size clay statue of a horse, on which the figure of Duke Francesco Sforza was later to have been placed. It was supposed to be cast in bronze but was first put on public view in Milan. Six years after Leonardo had modeled it, it had been neither finished nor cast. French soldiers then invading Milan decided to use the clay figure for target practice. They completely destroyed it.

Of the paintings attributed to Leonardo, many are unfinished. Several paintings said to be his are not his at all, or are partially his. His best, the *Last Supper* (see page 66), is in such terrible condition that it hardly serves as an example of the master's technique. This situation is mostly Leonardo's fault, for he executed the painting in a manner never before tried, and it started disintegrating quickly. To stimulate the vanishing process, the monks who lived in the monastery where the picture was done decided that they needed a new door in the room where it hung, and they cut the entrance through the bottom-center of the picture. Leonardo's most famous masterpiece has lasted but suffers, if possible, from too much fame. Reproductions of *Mona Lisa* (see page 67) hang everywhere: in classrooms, the dime store, the shoemaker's shop. Because of its exposure, nobody remembers when he first saw the painting, and everyone takes it for granted. Popular songs are sung about Mona Lisa, moustaches are painted on her, tourists want to see her. So, we are denied the excitement—so important in art—of discovery.

None of the architectural designs that Leonardo put on paper were built. Many of his inventions were too advanced to be produced with the materials and tools available in the fifteenth century. Yet, based on journals and sketches, a nonexistent statue, one barely existing painting, and another that suffers from over-exposure, the reputation of Leonardo da Vinci is equaled by only a handful of men throughout all of history. And that is how it should be.

Leonardo was the Renaissance man. He was all that his contemporaries wanted to be; he was all that his followers tried to be. His mind was ever open, and so were his eyes. He became an expert in any field that interested him. If you take a course in the history of mathematics, you pause to study Leonardo. In any book on astronomy or the history of industry or philosophy or anatomy, there are chapters on Leonardo. But first of all he belongs to art.

Leonardo is one of the few great heroes of history whose accomplishments are studied for their own sake; less has been written about his life. We admire others for their rebellious spirit, for their daring. Michelangelo's ability to produce great paintings that he didn't even want to do wins our affection. Who has not sympathized with Beethoven's deafness and admired his courage in producing his greatest music after the tragedy? But Leonardo's place is usually in the minds, not the hearts, of people. Perhaps this is because a man who accomplished so much seems superhuman. We look for a flaw and can't find it. In others we find bad temper, poverty, rejection by their contemporaries; in Leonardo we find a good-natured man, sought after by the best minds of his time, almost always successful, very nearly perfect.

The life of this great genius began in a village near the town of Vinci on April 15, 1452. His father was a successful notary and his mother, a peasant girl; they were not married. On his grandfather's farm Leonardo spent his early years, free to explore the nearby fields and streams. A gentle, handsome boy, he was fascinated by nature. He loved animals—especially horses and birds—but his affection was

as much scientific as emotional. It is well known that whenever he had money, the young master would go to a pet shop, buy as many birds as he could afford, and immediately set them free. (Apparently, this custom continued throughout his life.) He didn't like the idea of caging a bird, whose natural home was the tree and sky. But he also wanted to watch the way birds fly. As an adult, he tried to design a flying machine based on the actions of a bird's wings (see page 66).

It is uncertain when he first became interested in art, but Leonardo had achieved a local reputation before he was ten. While he was still in his boyhood, a peasant asked him to decorate a shield with a dragon, and the young artist agreed. In order to make the dragon look absolutely real, Leonardo took lizards, crickets, grasshoppers, snakes, and bats into his room. Choosing this part of one and that part of another, he contrived his dragon. Vasari wrote that it was one of the most frightening, ugly, yet masterful creatures ever to face a peasant's enemy.

When Leonardo was around sixteen, he moved with his father to Florence. Realizing that his son had great gifts, Ser Piero da Vinci apprenticed him to the Florentine painter and sculptor, Verrocchio (1435?–88), a fashionable and outstanding artist. Like most artists in the days of the apprenticeship system, Verrocchio took his teaching seriously. He demanded hard work and constant study, but to insist that Leonardo abandon his younger ideas about art was unthinkable. In 1476 Verrocchio allowed his pupil to paint one of the angels in his *Baptism of Christ*. According to legend, the angel was painted with such exquisite mastery that Verrocchio looked at it and gave up painting for good. The 55 facts seem to bear out the story, for there are indeed no Verrocchio paintings dated later than 1476.

Leonardo's incredible fame came to him while he was still young. Four years before painting the angel in the *Baptism,* he had been elected a master of the painter's guild. Gradually, more and more people learned of his skills, and by 1481 he was known all over Italy. In that year the monks of the important Saint Donato monastery near Florence commissioned him to paint their altarpiece. The artist made a great many drawings for this work, *The Adoration of the Kings.* Instead of working within the Italian tradition of showing the scene in a room or stable, Leonardo set it in a large landscape. To emphasize the importance of the Virgin and the kings, he employed chiaroscuro—the technique of sharply contrasting light and dark—to illuminate them.

Leonardo never finished the *Adoration.* We cannot be sure why he abandoned the project, but that he did is a clue to what some consider to be the master's one great flaw. The number of paintings begun by Leonardo is great; the number he finished is small. Why should such a genius have no apparent concern over his habit of not finishing what he started? Some scholars have suggested that he spread himself too thin, that a man who is a competent artist, mathematician, inventor, military strategist, and scientist cannot concentrate on any one field long enough to contribute as much as he is able. They conclude that had Leonardo spent all of his time working on his designs for the airplane, he might have succeeded in building it four hundred years before the Wright brothers. This opinion is not widely supported nowadays. First of all, with the materials then available, it is doubtful that even a workable design for an airplane could have been executed. On the matter of his having attempted too much, one must consider that Leonardo did not think of himself as "many different men." To Leonardo there was no difference between a geologist and a painter, for all things were rooted in science. Be it a painting or flying machine, his approach to it was the same: he examined the problem, sketched the possible solutions, decided on the most logical and workable, and made the product. Looking at it this way, there is, to be sure, no difference between a picture and a tank. Though their functions are separate, the process of creating each is identical. Therefore, it is likely that Leonardo regarded his unfinished paintings as scientifically complete. His preoccupation with other things did not prevent Leonardo from completing the *Adoration;* he simply stopped because he had solved the problem. He had given new life to the scene by his use of a perfectly balanced composition, chiaroscuro, and the landscape setting. After accomplishing this with his soft brown underpainting, he perhaps saw no need to continue. The addition of color would only have made the picture more conventionally— not more scientifically—complete. Later, such artists as Caravaggio and Rembrandt built up layers of brownish paint and used chiaroscuro to produce pictures that no one calls "unfinished."

Having decided not to go on with the *Adoration,* Leonardo wrote to Ludovico Sforza, Duke of Milan, seeking employment. The master's letter is a truly amazing document. Without boasting, he told the duke about his skills. In a matter-of-fact tone he called attention to his ability to design new weapons for war, map out both offensive and defensive battles, design public and private buildings, paint, sculpt, and build bridges. He concluded by offering to make the ill-fated statue of the duke's father. Leonardo frankly stated that he would not object to proving his extraordinary and varied ability in competition with the best men in each field. The duke would have been an idiot to refuse a position to the master.

During his eighteen years in Milan, Leonardo's genius became legendary. He performed all the duties he said he could as well as unexpected others. He supervised pageants, designed costumes, engineered the installation of central heating in the palace, entertained the duke and his friends by singing and playing the lute. Naturally, he composed the music himself. His chief artistic project during the first thirteen years was the statue. In connection with it, he made hundreds of exquisite drawings and wrote a book on the anatomy of the horse. Though Leonardo loved to dress well and enjoyed the luxury of court life, he apparently never put social pleasures above his work. To the master, work was his greatest pleasure.

Around 1496 Leonardo began planning his *Last Supper* (see detail page 66), which he painted in Santa Maria delle Grazie in Milan. The citizens of Milan grew accustomed to seeing Leonardo passing back and forth from his home to the monastery at any time of day or night. He was especially quiet during the two years when he was painting his masterpiece, and he worked very slowly and carefully. In the evening it was not unusual for him to get up from a half-eaten dinner, walk the two miles to the monastery, add two strokes to his work, and return to his meal.

The Last Supper was a subject that had been a favorite of Christian artists through the ages, and countless paintings of it exist from all periods. Leonardo—always one to look for the new in art—chose this often-illustrated scene to make one of his greatest innovations. Selecting the most dramatic part in the story, the artist depicted the event at the exact moment when Christ tells His disciples that one of them will betray Him. Each reacts in a different way, while Christ remains calm in the atmosphere of oncoming tragedy. The painting not only shows the scene, it projects the tension of the moment and describes the feelings of those involved. Though the science of psychology was unknown at the time, this interpretation has been described as a psychological one.

Most strongly affected by Christ's statement are St. Peter and Judas. Always easily angered, St. Peter clutches a knife in his hand; Judas, holding his purse containing the thirty pieces of silver he has received for his betrayal, draws back, astonished that his treachery has been found out. To give Judas the right kind of appearance, Leonardo spent considerable time studying and sketching the head of a criminal.

Leonardo liked fresco painting because it could be done on a wall, and oil painting because it made possible slow, thoughtful work. Therefore, he tried to paint in oils on a plaster wall. As a scientist, Leonardo must have known that oil and water do not mix, but he decided to experiment anyway. The wall was not well sealed and absorbed moisture whenever the weather became damp. As a result, the *Last Supper* began to deteriorate in the artist's lifetime—one of the great tragedies in art history. But the painting made its mark. Suddenly, other artists found themselves unable to paint a Last Supper. Leonardo had said it all; there was no reason to restate the subject. Not until Raphael introduced still newer approaches to subject matter did artists begin to paint the scene again. Except for Tintoretto, few were successful.

In the last year of the fifteenth century, the French invaded Milan and captured the duke. Easy as it is to detest the French troops for what they did to Leonardo's sculpture, it should be mentioned that the invasion was not without benefit, for the Sforza ruler had been one of the worst tyrants of the century.

Leonardo traveled through the North for a while, stopping in Venice just long enough to invent the diving bell and a swimming belt. Then, probably in 1500, he returned to Florence, where he was greeted with great enthusiasm. He experimented with paints again in his *Battle of Anghiari,* trying to revive the ancient medium known as *encaustic.* Almost immediately after it was applied, the encaustic paint, which is made of pigment and wax, ran down the wall— melted, actually, in the warmth of a sunny day. It is said that Michelangelo wept, that the city council pronounced the tragedy a state disaster, and that the whole population of Florence was beset by gloom.

Perhaps least affected by the catastrophe was the artist himself. Leonardo was disappointed, but as a scientist he knew that experimentation led to more failures than successes. Besides, he had already seen the wife of Francesco del Giocondo and was thinking about painting a portrait. There are many stories about the relationship between the artist and his model, but the truth is probably that Leonardo was interested in nothing more than the lovely face of the woman known as Mona Lisa.

She is the subject of a difficult work of art to talk about. Sitting, quietly smiling before a twilight landscape, she represents something never before created—and never equaled. But what was so new about her? Her smile? The smile had been painted well before, though it is one of the most difficult human expressions to depict with paint. Yet her smile is hers alone, and what she smiles about is her secret. Her hands? Small, folded in her lap, they are aristocratic, lovely, and seem to live on the canvas. Looking at them closely, one sees that they were painted simply, with little detail. Still, they seem to live. Or is it her eyes, which appear to look through ours?

Reproductions cannot reveal the delicacy of Leonardo's brushstroke. There are no clear outlines, for the master blended one line into the next. So skillful was he with the still-young medium that one cannot help but wish that he had painted everything in oil.

Florence wanted Leonardo to repaint his melted battle scene, but the *Mona Lisa* had made him impatient with the subject. Taking his masterpiece with him, he left for Milan and never returned to Florence. For the French viceroy in Milan he painted two outstanding pictures: *The Virgin of the Rocks* (see page 65), painted with a student, and *St. Anne with the Virgin and the Infant Christ,* which he never finished. They were his last great pictures.

At sixty Leonardo went to Rome. Pope Leo X was accustomed to the great number of paintings produced by Raphael and his assistants. He could not accept the slowness and constant interruptions that were Leonardo's habit, and the artist found little work there. After two years he responded to an invitation of Francis I of France, who gave the artist a lovely home in Touraine and demanded little other than Leonardo's presence.

His hands became paralyzed and he could no longer paint. He had brought the *Mona Lisa* with him, and he apparently did not mourn his inability to produce pictures. Comfortable, at peace in his country home, he didn't let his mind become paralyzed, and his admiring visitors listened with gratitude as they heard the words of one of the most brilliant men who ever lived. At sixty-seven, on May 1, 1519, he died.

Raphael

So bright was the light of the age that it shone over art for generations. New styles formed and faded—mannerism, baroque, rococo, neo-classicism—but the roots of all were planted firmly in the Renaissance.

To later artists it was Raphael who symbolized the peak of Renaissance painting. Students were ordered to copy his drawing and imitate his compositions. Museums placed his pictures in solitary rooms so that viewers would not be distracted by lesser works. Throughout the world of art, the name of Raphael was regarded with almost religious awe.

Raphael was given credit for nearly everything good that developed under the influence of Renaissance style. Therefore, when the time for a break came, he was blamed for everything bad. In the nineteenth century a number of artists thought that the classical influence had lasted too long. It was a time of great social revolution. Turning against classical formality, with its glorification of godlike heroes and ideal beauty, these artists wanted to capture the beauty they saw in the humility and honesty of simple people. It was natural for them to reject the painter whose work typified the view opposite theirs. Gustave Courbet (1819–77), a leader of the new group, left no doubt about his feelings. Given the chance, he said, he would punch Raphael in the mouth. An organization of English painters began placing the initials PRB after their signatures. After two years of secrecy, they revealed that the letters stood for "Pre-Raphaelite Brotherhood."

Thus friends and foes alike placed Raphael in the center of art history—sort of a Mason-Dixon line separating old from new. His pictures tell stories with beauty and clarity, and his followers thought this was the purpose of art. But his critics in the nineteenth century wanted art rich with noble ideas. They thought his work too pretty and shallow and his influence harmful.

If Courbet had known Raphael, the chances are that he would not have wanted to punch him at all. In fact, Raphael probably would have listened courteously to Courbet's objections and tried to satisfy the Frenchman. Raphael was not well suited to being at the center of controversy. He was too polite, too friendly, too anxious to please.

Vasari wrote that Raphael was, "among so many beautiful, the most beautiful. . . ." The writer was speaking of everything about the artist: his creative powers, his temperament, his face, his heart and soul. A master of his art, Raphael was also a master of his conscience. He won the affection of Popes and beggars, whom he treated with equal courtesy and generosity.

His uncle, the architect Donato Bramante (1444–1514), 63

often acted without Raphael's knowledge as a kind of publicity agent for the artist. Inclined to deride the art of others in order to secure work for his nephew, Bramante managed to make a few enemies for Raphael. This greatly upset the master, who then made every effort to patch up the relationships. Friendship was important to him; indeed, it would be his downfall.

He was born Raphaello Sanzio on March 28, 1483, in the little Italian town of Urbino. His father, Giovanni, was a modestly accomplished painter who operated one of the most prosperous workshops in the province of Umbria. Young Raphaello from his boyhood worked in the shop; he was one of the few Italian Renaissance masters who never served an apprenticeship period away from home.

By the time he was twelve, both his parents had died. Giovanni's workshop, however, continued to prosper; and Raphael remained to work alongside the other artists. His treatment there had an important effect on his early work.

Raphael was kept busy and was a hard worker; nevertheless, his life was easy and peaceful. The other artists treated him as a younger brother, responding to his simplest wishes. Another boy in the same circumstances might have been spoiled rotten; Raphael was spoiled gentle (but spoiled he was). He was not forceful because he never had to be. That he did not know the meaning of struggle, tension, and strength of will is clear in his early paintings. He discovered this himself, and throughout his career he attempted to add these qualities to his work. To learn how, he was a constant student of artists whose work was more forceful than his.

64 It is well known to art historians that Raphael was very

opposite: Leonardo da Vinci. *The Virgin of the Rocks.*

Louvre, Paris

Leonardo da Vinci. *The Last Supper* (detail).   *Santa Maria delle Grazie, Milan*

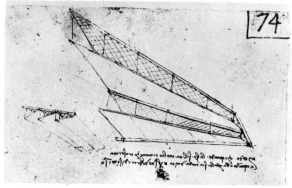

Details from the drawings of Leonardo da Vinci

Leonardo da Vinci. *Mona Lisa.*   *Louvre, Paris*

Michelangelo. *The Creation.*   *Detail of the Sistine ceiling, The Vatican*

Michelangelo. *The Fall of Man.*   *Detail of the Sistine ceiling, The Vatican*

opposite: Michelangelo. Interior of the Sistine Chapel.

The Vatican   69

Raphael. *Madonna Granduca.*

Pitti Palace, Florence

Raphael. *School of Athens.*

Stanza del Segnatura, The Vatican

Raphael. *Marriage of the Virgin.*   *Brera Gallery, Milan*

Michelangelo. *The Holy Family.*　　　*Uffizi Gallery, Florence*

easily influenced. Apparently, the artist deliberately allowed these influences to affect him.

In 1500 Raphael went to the town of Perugia to join the workshop of Perugino (1445?–1523). It is probable that the two artists were colleagues and did not have (as was once thought) a formal teacher-student relationship.

But Raphael did learn from Perugino. Perugino had been a student of Piero della Francesca. Despite the fact that Piero's work was already considered old-fashioned, Raphael was impressed with the geometric, orderly, almost architectural compositions that Piero employed. Raphael arranged his backgrounds in much the same way, but he was not willing to have his figures serve as supporting elements in an architectural scheme. In contrast to the figures in Piero's work, the people in Raphael's pictures are of primary importance. They actually enact the event as though they were players performing their roles before an architectural backdrop.

Sposalizio, which the master painted when he was twenty-one, reveals the direction that Raphael's work would take. Above all else, Raphael was a teller of stories. In *Sposalizio* he tells his story as a playwright might, using players and scenery. Later, he would change his style and approach, but only to make his stories clearer, the better to describe the painted event.

In 1504 Raphael went to Florence. The young artist was overwhelmed by the work of Leonardo and Michelangelo. He studied their work in depth, looked at his own, and realized his limitations. He saw that although he had captured the grace and beauty of religious figures, he had failed to suggest their great strength and sacrifices. He had given saints the painted beauty of actors instead of the soulful beauty that comes from struggle and determination. He had described miracles as though they were successful business deals. He realized that because of his upbringing he had taken accomplishment for granted.

During his nearly four years in Florence, Raphael painted a series of Madonnas (see pages 70 and 107). His increasing grasp of the works of Leonardo and Michelangelo is clear. Michelangelo had not yet painted at that time, but Raphael made sketches of his sculpture. Setting out to achieve with paint the dramatic force of Michelangelo's stone giants, Raphael still retained his own qualities. His Marys and Jesuses grew stronger, more like the determined figures they really must have been. But Raphael continued to tell his stories simply and clearly. The figures were still gentle and delicate, their grace expressed as Raphael alone could express it.

From Leonardo, Raphael learned a great deal about technique. Analyzing Leonardo's pictures, he discovered that this master of masters constructed paintings as whole units. His own works had been put together part by part. In the *Sposalizio,* for example, the temple was the backdrop, the stairs and plaza the stage, and the main characters the actors; each formed a different and completely independent unit. Realizing that no such distinction was apparent in Leonardo's work, Raphael studied the master's sketchbooks and filled his own with preparatory drawings. Excluding small details, he hoped to achieve such unity that the entire picture would be dependent on all the parts, and that no one part could exist without the whole. He also examined Leonardo's use of color and, as a result, learned to make his own crisper and more gemlike.

In 1508 Raphael returned to Urbino to work for the Duke of Umbria. His stay was brief, however, for Pope Julius II summoned him to Rome. A brilliant, powerful Pontiff (with whom we will become better acquainted in the chapter on Michelangelo), Julius was largely responsible for making the Vatican the glorious place it is. Demanding the best of everything for the Church, he did with the Vatican for Rome what Lorenzo de Medici had done with his palace garden for Florence. Indeed, the center of Renaissance activity shifted to Rome. The age entered a new phase, which the men of the time called the High Renaissance.

Raphael's first assignment was to fresco the Stanza del Segnatura, the Pope's official office-library. On the ceiling the artist painted symbolic illustrations of the four faculties: Theology, Jurisprudence (law), Philosophy, and Poetry. On the four walls are pictures that give examples of each faculty put to excellent use. For example, *Parnassus* is the mural that illustrates poetry. It shows a convention of poets with the mythical god Apollo as chairman and the Muses as officers. *School of Athens* (see page 70), exemplifying philosophy, shows a similar meeting over which Plato and Aristotle preside.

Because Julius was so impressed with Raphael, he had works by other artists elsewhere in the Vatican destroyed so that Raphael could repaint them. In another *stanza* the artist depicted the history of the Church; in a third, he illustrated a great Papal miracle. He decorated the Loggia 75 (porch) at the Vatican and, in 1514, was asked to design ten tapestries for the Sistine Chapel. Appointed chief archi- tect of St. Peter's Basilica that same year, Raphael was also made official guardian of the ancient ruins of Rome. As his fame and wealth increased, he was also given more private commissions. He decorated town palaces and country homes, designed tombs, and painted glorious portraits. Wealthy Romans yearned to own his splendid easel pictures (paint- ings executed with no regard for the setting in which they may be placed). Raphael, incidentally, was greatly respon- sible for the replacement of mural painting by easel paint- ing as the dominant form of art—a dominance that exists to this day. His output was tremendous, and he worked harder and harder. He worked himself up to the top of his profes- sion, then went over the top and into a tragically early grave.

Raphael's human flaw was that he just could not say no. Julius had given him a lifetime of work. It was not the Pope's fault that the artist tried to complete that work so quickly. Raphael was admired for his work and for his own personal qualities; therefore the wealthy aristocrats of Rome wanted him and no one else to work for them. They also were eager to share his company. Because they were his personal friends, Raphael would not refuse their commis- sions. This situation led to his artistic flaws.

Left with no other choice, Raphael hired assistants—a great many of them. This was quite normal in those days, but the master had to allow his helpers too much respon- sibility. Many lacked talent or maturity, or both. As a re- sult, Raphael's huge output included too large a proportion of mediocre and downright bad pictures. Every master produces unworthy works, but most throw the lesser ones away. Raphael would not allow himself this luxury.

It is important to understand that Raphael was his own worst enemy. Genuinely fond of the lavishness of Roman social life, he participated in it as though he were a gentleman of leisure. Much of his time was spent at his tailor's being fitted for his fashionable wardrobe. He accepted invitations to almost every important dinner party. After dining on foods that were too rich, he remained for long hours, sipping robust Italian wine, talking about art and literature with his friends.

But he was not a gentleman with time for so much leisure. After his long social nights he slept little if at all; and early every morning he was scurrying about from palace to villa, from studio to the Vatican, supervising his helpers, fulfilling his many obligations.

According to a rumor (probably based on truth), he found time for brief meetings with a baker's daughter, with whom he was apparently very much in love. She was not part of Roman high society, which he also loved, so the meetings were secret. Raphael was in fact for many years engaged to the Pope's niece. He avoided marriage, though, protesting that it would be unfair to take a wife to whom he could devote so little time. He pledged to reduce his load of work but never did; in any case it seems that he did not love her and used his work as an excuse to repeatedly postpone the wedding without insulting her important family.

The weight of work and social life was heavy. His strenuous activity and irregular hours and unwise diet weakened his body. A body so abused loses its ability to resist illness. Ra- 77 phael frequently caught colds; one got gradually worse and turned to fever. The best care in Rome was provided him. For ten days he lay in bed fighting the high temperatures burning through his body. On Good Friday, April 6, 1520, he lost the fight.

His funeral might have been that of a Caesar or Pope. Romans jammed the streets for a final tribute.

"He must have known that he would die young," they said. "That is why he worked to complete a lifetime's work in thirty-seven years."

The truth, of course, is just the opposite. Raphael completed a lifetime's work in thirty-seven years. That is why he died so young.

Michelangelo

On March 6, 1475, when his fourth son was born, Judge Buonarroti stepped out of his hillside house near Florence and looked at the nighttime sky. A superstitious man, he was certain that the stars revealed a lucky sign. With pride and hope he re-entered the house and announced that his new son's name would be Michelangelo, after Michael the archangel, a great heavenly warrior. Then he waited anxiously for his son to grow up.

From the start it seemed to the family that something had been wrong with the sky on Michelangelo's birthnight. Small and sickly, whining and coughing his way through childhood, the boy gave no indication that his future might be worthy of his name. Although he was sent to the best schools and received tutoring in military and political matters, Michelangelo distressed the family. Not only was his health poor, but he was stubborn and unsociable and wasted his time drawing. His father and uncles beat him, insisting that he study. When beatings failed they tried reason: heaven itself, they told him, had made it clear that he was intended to serve his country as a general or statesman. Michelangelo continued to draw. Reason having failed, they tried beatings again.

When the artist was about thirteen, Michelangelo's father —it must have been with a great sigh—finally gave up hope and agreed to let the boy study with a popular Florentine painter, Domenico Ghirlandaio (1449–94). In Ghirlandaio's workshop Michelangelo's life, but not his temperament, changed. As a boy he had been stubborn and quick to anger, and in the studio he was as hard to get along with as ever. But before he had been surrounded by stupidity, and now he was in the company of intelligent people. He continued to argue with anyone about any subject, but now the views that opposed his were often reasonable. It is easy to rise above the prejudices of the ignorant; it is more difficult to overcome the objections of the intelligent. It took a genius like Michelangelo to disagree with so many good minds, to make so many sound opinions change, to turn his enemies into his champions, to become a hero first to his contemporaries and countrymen and then to people of all lands.

Even at thirteen Michelangelo abused other artists, most of whom were much older. Before whiskers grew on his face, he had made enemies of his fellow-students and probably of Ghirlandaio himself. Perhaps they were jealous of his talent. Perhaps they knew that they could never equal 79 the goal that Michelangelo had set for himself—the achievement of perfection in art—and that Michelangelo probably would. Perhaps they would have disliked him for these reasons alone. But Michelangelo constantly and bitterly criticized their work, and that made him intolerable. Though they would worship him later, they hated him then.

Ghirlandaio taught Michelangelo the fresco technique but little else. He was either a lazy teacher (which is doubtful, since he had many students from important families) or he realized that the extraordinary genius of Michelangelo might better be developed in surroundings with more able competition. Although Ghirlandaio could have employed the talent of Michelangelo in his workshop, the teacher sent his student to the Medici garden.

The second teacher of Michelangelo was Bertoldo de Giovanni (1420?–91), one of the great sculptors of fifteenth-century Florence. During his years with Bertoldo at the Medici Palace, Michelangelo found himself deeply involved with sculpture, and he came to love the art far more than he would ever love painting.

One day (according to a sixteenth-century account) Lorenzo de Medici was walking in his garden and came upon Michelangelo carving a mask. Jokingly, the prince commented that he thought it strange that the face was supposed to be that of a very old man, yet it had all its teeth. Several days later Lorenzo returned to see Michelangelo, after having removed a tooth in the mask, altering the gum to look as though the tooth had been lost from the roots because of old age. Lorenzo didn't laugh. Impressed with the young artist's 80 skill and his concern with accuracy and detail, the prince instructed Michelangelo to notify his father to come to the Medici Palace.

Judge Buonarroti had not changed. To him the promise of the stars had never been kept. When Lorenzo told him that Michelangelo would from then on be supported by the Medici, the aged judge burst into tears. Another parent's tears would have been tears of joy, but not his. Sadder than ever, too insensitive to understand or appreciate art, Buonarroti lived to see his son become the most famous artist in the world. Eventually Michelangelo supported the whole family well. But to his father, Michelangelo was never anything more than a lowly stonecutter.

Treated as a member of the Medici family, Michelangelo was given a large allowance and the right to use any part of the palace. He was even permitted to wear the purple robe that indicated aristocracy. Lorenzo saw to it that Michelangelo was introduced to the most famous men of the day and encouraged the boy to participate in their discussions. Through these sessions, Michelangelo learned much about Greek and Roman philosophy and came to admire the classical attempt to describe ideal forms in art. At night he studied anatomy and secretly cut up dead bodies that he had bought to see how they were put together.

Michelangelo was considered one of the royal family, but his behavior hardly matched his position. His criticism of others did not stop, his manners remained characteristically bad, and his temper was as hot as ever. In spite of himself, however, and in spite of his youth, his reputation spread. Florence was taking him to its heart. He never sought the position, but he was becoming a hero.

The intense love for Michelangelo that the Florentines had is well illustrated by the story of an unfortunate young sculptor named Pietro Torrigiano (1472–1528). Torrigiano was a talented student in the Medici garden. Like Michelangelo and the others, he often went to the Church of the Carmine to study the chapel decorated by Masaccio. As was his habit, Michelangelo spent as much time abusing the drawings of others as he spent making his own, and Torrigiano grew to despise him. One day, according to Torrigiano's own diary, "I got more angry than usual, and, clenching my fist, I gave him such a blow on the nose that I felt bone and cartilage go down like a biscuit beneath my knuckles; and this mark of mine he will carry with him to the grave." When Torrigiano broke Michelangelo's nose, he gave himself a much worse mark, one that he, too, carried with him to the grave, and one that caused him much more agony. His friends—even those who had claimed to hate Michelangelo—stopped talking to him. Fearing punishment from Lorenzo, he fled Florence. All Florentines came to hate his name, and whenever he returned he was met with silence and frequently threats. Many years later, Torrigiano found work in England but needed helpers. The talented young master Benvenuto Cellini (1500–1578) was interested and was about to accept when he found out who Torrigiano was. Torrigiano had to look elsewhere. The sculptor had been young and angry when he broke Michelangelo's nose, but this one act of violence blemished his name for life. He was hated until and after his death; indeed, there are few less popular names in Florence today than that of Torrigiano the nose-breaker.

Michelangelo left Florence soon after the death of Lorenzo in 1492. After traveling through Italy for a few years, he arrived in Rome. There he created his first major work, an exquisite statue, *Pietà,* completed in 1499, which made him world-famous. He returned to Florence in 1501 and began to work on a magnificent statue that he carved from a long, scarred piece of marble which other sculptors had rejected. When this work, *David,* was unveiled in 1504, the citizens of Florence adopted the statue of this youthful warrior as a symbol of the strength and vigor of their city. Anyone with money wanted Michelangelo to carve whatever he needed carved. The artist was commissioned to do much more work than he could possibly finish.

When Michelangelo was thirty, the longest and most bitterly waged battle of his life began. Like many feuds between great men, the one that Michelangelo had with Pope Julius II is fascinating; for it is difficult to tell whether the two men actually loved or hated each other. They fought with passion, causing themselves and each other much agony, yet Julius continued to demand that Michelangelo work for him, and the artist worked on the Pope's tomb long after Julius's death.

It started in 1505. Julius chose Michelangelo to design and sculpt the largest tomb in the Christian world. It was to be so huge that a new chapel would be needed at St. Peter's Basilica to contain it. Michelangelo, who seldom trusted anyone to make decisions regarding his work, spent eight months at the marble quarry supervising the selection of stone for the project. When he returned to Rome to discuss details with Julius, Michelangelo was told that the Pope was 83 too busy to see him. Furious, Michelangelo refused to wait and went back to Florence.

Michelangelo's fury was matched by the anger of the Pope. Julius was a tough, frank, brilliant Pontiff, who had no use for courtly manners and no patience with those who challenged his absolute power. He was hard and immovable in his dealings with all who served him, for he felt that the Church must be strong and in total control of the Christian world. Julius was the most powerful and important living Christian; Michelangelo was the greatest living artist; the Pope would settle for nothing less than the best. He ordered Michelangelo to return to Rome. When Michelangelo refused, Julius threatened to send troops to Florence, and if necessary destroy the city to find the artist. Not wanting to be the cause of the destruction of Florence, Michelangelo agreed to return to Rome and finished his work. It took him forty years.

While Michelangelo was working on the tomb he was interrupted frequently. The most important interruption occurred between 1508 and 1512. One day Julius approached Michelangelo at his work and commanded him to paint the ceiling of the Sistine Chapel (which is part of St. Peter's at the Vatican) (see pages 68, 69). Again the artist lost his temper. Painting, he protested, was not his trade; the job should be given to Raphael. The Pope replied that he, not Michelangelo, was the best judge of ability. Beside himself with anger, Michelangelo put aside his work on the tomb and began planning this tremendous project, muttering all the while.

Michelangelo said that he hated painting. He once commented that it was a woman's work. Yet he worked as hard and consistently on the project as he had ever worked before. An architect named Bramante designed the scaffolding on which the artist would labor. Perhaps the scaffolds were poorly designed—Bramante hated Michelangelo—but, in any case, the artist took one look at the construction and ordered it taken apart. He then designed his own unit that would support him as comfortably as possible. Moreover, the scaffolds were erected in such a way that allowed Michelangelo to stand on the Chapel floor and view all parts of the painting through the beams.

At first Michelangelo hired assistants, but when he saw their work he ordered them out and locked the Chapel doors so that they would not return. Complaining constantly about the Pope's refusal to send him more money, and reminding everyone he saw that painting was not his art, Michelangelo nevertheless began to spend more and more time in the Chapel. His excitement grew. He slept in his clothing to save time. He had to lie on his back while painting, and that must have caused pain; but he took no holidays and rested very seldom.

When the painting on the ceiling was only half finished, Julius, ignoring the artist's protest, decided to open the Chapel for the public to see. In the crush of mobs coming to view their hero's work, there were several deaths, and Julius ordered the Chapel closed again. But among the visitors had been Bramante and his nephew Raphael. Bramante tried to convince the Pope that Raphael, who had no objection to working with assistants, could finish the job in half the time it would take Michelangelo. When Julius informed Michelangelo of Bramante's suggestion, the master said that he would tolerate no interference from Raphael.

For once the Pope supported Michelangelo, who went back to work, alone as before.

Day after day for more than a year Julius returned to see how the ceiling was progressing. One day he shouted up to Michelangelo, asking when he planned to finish the project. The artist called back that he would finish when he could. Infuriated, the Pope screamed, "When you can! Do you want me to throw you down from this scaffold?" He stormed out. As soon as the Pope had gone, Michelangelo climbed down and ordered the scaffolding taken apart. Someone ran after Julius and told him; he rushed back, insisting that more work be done, but the artist said he was through. The Pope objected that without gold trimming, the work would look poor. Michelangelo is said to have pointed out that the people in the painted Biblical scenes were, in real life, poor, too. Julius smiled and blessed Michelangelo.

A year later Julius died, and Michelangelo continued to work on the Pope's tomb. Perhaps Michelangelo remembered when Julius had overruled his objections to painting the Sistine ceiling, saying, "I am the one to estimate your abilities." Apparently this statement was not a product of the Pope's conceit alone; for the ceiling represents what is probably the most colossal achievement by one man in the history of painting. Yet it was accomplished by a master sculptor who, at least publicly, never ceased to regard the art of painting with contempt.

Covering thousands of square feet, the Sistine ceiling is carefully organized and skillfully painted. The Old Testament figures—there are 343 of them—range from life-size to eighteen feet in height. The scenes describe the drama of man, beginning with the creation of the world and ending with the salvation of man through the sacrifice of Christ. Michelangelo selected the more familiar scenes in Biblical history. First we see God laboring to divide lightness from darkness. Then He creates the moon and stars and separates the earth from the sea. Finally, in a beautifully painted scene, God creates man and woman. In the next set of scenes, *The Fall of Man* (see page 69), the serpent persuades Eve to take the forbidden apple; she and Adam bite it and are driven from Eden. The Fall climaxes with the flood and sacrifice of Noah. Man and beast have been spared, and the drama is now ready for man's total salvation.

The event is prophesied by seven Hebrew prophets and five Greek and Roman sibyls, who foretell the coming of Christ. They are shown seated, clutching oak leaves from which hang pictures of Old Testament stories. The pictures look like ancient bronze reliefs. The part in the drama that will be played by the Church is suggested in the twelve lunettes (round pictures), portraying the ancestors of Christ.

Four triangular panels depict earlier miracles of salvation: the rescue of the Jews by David when he kills the giant Goliath; by Judith when she kills the enemy King Holofernes and carries his head away in a sack; by Esther when she secures the execution of the tyrant Haman; and by Moses when he fashions the brazen serpent to drive away the snakes that were killing his people.

Very little background detail exists on the Sistine paintings. Michelangelo concentrated on the human figure, which he regarded as divine. The figures of the wingless angels, especially, show the artist's ideal of a body untouched by the blemishes produced by sin. He much preferred the muscular, tight-skinned body of the male to that of the female; and

most of his women have the bodies of men, softened somewhat, and with breasts added. The female faces, however,

are feminine and often quite lovely.

The Sistine ceiling is a vast hymn in praise of man as God's most marvelous creation. This idea, which Michelangelo expressed so magnificently, was one of the cornerstones of Renaissance thought and marked the chief difference in attitude between that period and the Middle Ages.

For twenty-four years after the completion of the Sistine ceiling, Michelangelo did no painting. Then, in 1536, Pope Paul III called upon the artist to paint a companion piece to the ceiling. For seven years he worked on *The Last Judgment* (see page 68), a giant mural above the altar of the Sistine Chapel. The painting of this mural matches the quality of the ceiling pictures; but, obviously, Michelangelo's attitude had changed. Corrupt and lazy, the leaders of Italy had been unable to resist invasion by foreign troops. The country had declined, and the curiosity and excitement of discovery that characterized the Renaissance were fast being replaced by apathy and self-satisfaction. By looking at *The Last Judgment* we can tell that Michelangelo was no longer the faithful believer in humanity that he had once been. Although his style remained similar, his attitude was more medieval. The mural is filled with activity, with people clearly worried about how they will be judged. Sinners in hell are grotesque and pathetic.

Michelangelo was sixty-seven when he finished *The Last Judgment;* apparently he remained as hot-tempered and stubborn as he had been as a youth. He had gained a sense
88   of humor, but that, too, was a tool he used against others.

A man named Biagio da Cesena, a minor official in the Pope's court, was very much opposed to Michelangelo's handling of *The Last Judgment*. Cesena especially criticized the naked figures in the painting and felt they should be clothed. Michelangelo responded by immortalizing his critic in paint. When the mural was unveiled, visitors saw among the miserable creatures in hell the face of Biagio da Cesena.

Every once in a while Michelangelo would decide to paint. Generally, he would abandon his picture soon after starting it. The only easel painting that he is known to have completed is *The Holy Family* (see page 72). In the Uffizi Gallery in Florence there is a picture of Michelangelo, but we are not certain whether it is a self-portrait. It probably is, for it seems unlikely that the artist would have given another the courtesy of posing.

The Vatican frequently needed enlargement and change. In 1547 Michelangelo was appointed chief architect of St. Peter's. The dome he designed for the basilica has often been called the crown of the Renaissance. It has been widely copied.

He lived to be eighty-nine It was said that during his last years he could still carve faster and better than three ordinary sculptors. He worked steadily until his death in Rome on February 18, 1565.

Rembrandt came along to challenge the master's first rank among painters. Bernini took up where Michelangelo left off as an architect-designer. No sculptor has been able to capture the strength and vigor of Michelangelo's work. Rodin—to whom the master was an unapproachable hero—came close. But as a complete artist, Michelangelo stands alone. The stars were right after all.

THE HIGH RENAISSANCE
IN VENICE

Giorgione

Titian

Tintoretto

Many scholars and artists—Vasari among them—thought that the Renaissance reached its peak after 1490. They believed that the work of Leonardo, Raphael, and Michelangelo summed up all the experimentation and discovery that had characterized fifteenth-century Florence. Thus they came to call the first quarter of the sixteenth century the High Renaissance. Rome was its capital.

But, as we have seen, not all was well in Rome. The optimism that typified Renaissance thinking was giving way to disillusionment—and for good reason. The decaying politics of central Italy reversed the social progress of a century. Exactly one hundred years after the Medici had become rulers of Florence, marking the beginning of an era that affected 90 all Italy, the troops of Charles V of Spain sacked Rome.

This was in 1527; and from then on the Renaissance spirit in Florence and Rome was all but strangled. The change in attitude can be seen in *The Last Judgment*. Michelangelo's great mural does not really belong to the Renaissance. Its style marks the start of a new trend called *mannerism*, which will be described later.

In the second quarter of the sixteenth century, the center of Renaissance activity shifted from Florence and Rome to Venice. Because Venice was spared most of the turmoil that was making the rest of Italy a plaything in the hands of the Spanish and French, many Italian and foreign artists went there. Moreover, Venice had its own traditions of painting. And just as Florence and Rome had seen so many masters active at once, Venice was about to enter its golden age.

The land called Venetia, of which Venice is the seaport, was an independent state. It was somewhat removed from the affairs of Europe for reasons both geographic and economic. To the west were the Alps, to the east Asia Minor, to the south the Adriatic Sea. Venetians were in a good position to travel and do business with their neighbors, but when circumstances demanded, they could retreat to their well-protected homeland. From the standpoint of geography, the invasion of Venetia would have been difficult, even with huge forces.

But there was an even more important reason why foreign countries would hesitate to make enemies of the Venetians. Venice was the gateway between the East and the West. Through the seaport passed fine fabrics, precious jewels, ivory and jade exported from the Orient to Europe. Therefore, from the standpoint of economics, the loss of Venice's good will could have been disastrous for many nations. The Vene- 91

tians were merchants and bankers to the world; they knew
their business well, and their trade contributed much to the
prosperity of their friends.

Venice was a rich and colorful city. Built on a network
of lagoons and canals, it was as bright as a carnival. The
merchant barons who ruled built great churches and palaces
in architectural styles that combined the most colorful elements of East and West. State holidays crowded the calen-
dar, and the city was a center for drama, opera, and festivals
of all kinds. In civic pride and participation, Venetians were
second to none. Laws were even passed requiring ships to
return with at least one ornament suitable for the decoration
of the city's buildings and plazas.

The ideas of the Italian Renaissance reached Venice early,
and the Venetians embraced them happily. But there were
a number of differences between Venice and the rest of Italy
that are important to know. First, the Venetians were much
less religious than the Florentines and Romans. They belonged to the Roman Church, but they were far away from
the Pope. While ruling families of central Italy, such as the
Medici, Rovere, and Borghese, used their political powers
to control the Church, the merchant barons of Venice had no
special desire to dominate the Vatican. Second, Venetian art
developed out of a truly international heritage. The Italian
Renaissance in Florence had come, for the most part, from
the study of classical art and grew as a reaction against European medievalism. But the Venetians were less conscious of
ancient Greco-Roman art and were greatly influenced by
Byzantine art. When they adopted the ideas of the Renaissance, they did not attempt to discard their medieval-Byzan-
tine traditions. Third, Venetians were less scientific and

scholarly than were the founders of Renaissance thought. They were not nearly so interested in profound ideas, and were much more concerned with pageantry and, in their art, decorative quality.

The differences between Florentine-Roman and Venetian art can be seen when you compare the paintings of the fifteenth century Florentines discussed earlier with those of the Bellini family of Venice. Jacopo Bellini (1400?–1470?) owned the most productive workshop in fifteenth-century Venice. Jacopo visited Florence and learned much about Renaissance painting, then taught his two sons, Gentile (1429?–1507) and Giovanni (1433?–1516) (see pages 108–110). The Bellini adopted the perspective and anatomy systems employed in Florence, but their paintings remained typically Venetian. While Masaccio had emphasized his subject's emotions and Piero had stressed order and unity, the Bellini concentrated on decorative composition, the pageantry of whole scenes, and color. In contrast to the muted, sharply separated hues favored by the Florentines, the Bellini preferred rich, softly blended, jewel-like color.

Paint has much to do with the development of painting styles. The Flemish—perhaps as early as the fourteenth century—had invented oil paint. Through the travels of Jan van Eyck (birthdate unknown; died 1441 or 1442), the medium had been taught to the Italians. Until Raphael, oil paint was not widely employed in central Italy, but the Venetians were attracted to it at once. Much time was spent in the Bellini workshop experimenting with the new medium.

It has been suggested that the difference between the Florentine and Venetian techniques is due to the latter's use of oil paint. It is true that egg tempera and fresco, which the 93

Florentines employed, are much less versatile than oil. The older media are transparent and dry very quickly. Oil, on the other hand, can be made transparent or opaque, can be applied thickly or thinly. Because it dries very slowly, wet paint on the brush can be worked into wet paint on the surface; edges may be easily softened or blended together. Red may disappear into brown, and from the brown, a blue may emerge so subtly that the point at which the color changes is invisible. But the suggestion that paint alone separates the Florentine technique from the Venetian seems absurd when you consider what did happen when the central Italians finally began to use oil.

The technique of Raphael, for example, was in the Florentine tradition; and he often used oil paint. But Raphael's colors, like the colors of early Florentines, were localized. This means that each area of color was independent of the others. (Working in a children's coloring book requires the application of localized colors.) Raphael used oil because he liked the feel of it and many of its features—but he did not take advantage of the medium's blending qualities.

Strange as it may seem, the differences in the two approaches to painting caused—long after the Renaissance—a split among painters. Sometimes the split erupted into major quarrels. In the eighteenth and nineteenth centuries in France, the neoclassical painters who had belonged to the French Academy of Art employed the Florentine approach of localizing colors. Their bitter enemies, the so-called Romantics, Realists, and Impressionists, followed the Venetian lead and blended colors. The Florentine technique came to be called academic (after the Academy), and the Venetian technique, painterly. Even in the twentieth century the division exists, though not so bitterly. Abstract painting is often classified as to whether it is "hard-edged" (localized color) or "soft-edged" (painterly).

In the sixteenth century the Venetians began to use two-point perspective. The Florentines had used one-point perspective. The difference between the two systems seems, at first, to be just a technical one. Actually, the difference goes deeper than technique and suggests a wholly different attitude about the function of a picture and the role of the viewer.

According to the rules of perspective, all parallel receding lines, if continued indefinitely, are drawn as though they would meet at the horizon. In the Florentine system, all such receding lines meet at a single point, usually located at the center of vision. Earlier in this book a railroad track was given as an example of one-point perspective.

In the Venetian system, receding parallel lines meet at two points on the horizon. These vanishing points are located at the extremes of vision; that is, at the widest points that the human eye can perceive. A cube drawn in one-point perspective looks like this:

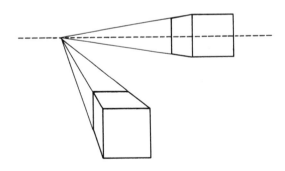

And a cube drawn in two-point perspective looks like this:

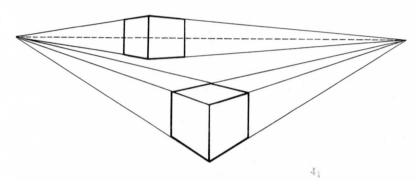

One- and two-point perspective have entirely different effects on the viewer. The older system tends to draw the viewer into the action of the painting. In most cases, for example, architectural settings were used to border and embrace the painted activity. The lines of the architecture project outward from a central point. This has the effect of placing the viewer at the corner of a street on which the action is taking place. All the viewer has to do to be in the middle of everything is to take a few steps.

Looking at a picture painted with two-point perspective is more like standing at a distance, watching the action without getting involved in it. The activity that is closest may occur anywhere on the canvas; but from that point all the detail fades into the distance. In the one-point system figures move about within their setting, and that setting embraces us as well as the principal characters. In most two-point perspective, activity takes place in front of its setting; the figures could be compared to actors performing in front of painted scenery.

Two-point perspective is more accurate than one-point.

The Florentine and Roman artists knew this as well as the Venetians. Despite the fact that they were more deeply concerned with scientific and intellectual matters, the artists of central Italy were willing to sacrifice absolute accuracy in order to involve the viewer in their work. In contrast, the Venetians—perhaps because of their Eastern heritage—were more interested in achieving decorative patterns and describing the relationships between shapes and spaces. They wanted to capture the over-all movement of a panoramic scene. That their system of perspective was more accurate is of minor importance.

Can you see the differences in effectiveness of the two perspective systems? In the drawings below, the silhouettes represent the viewer:

The Bellini dominated Venetian painting in the fifteenth century. Their world-famous workshop attracted many foreign artists to Venice, and they made Venice very much a part of the Italian Renaissance. So, when it was called upon to take the lead in the continuation of Renaissance painting, Venice was ready.

Unfortunately, most of Giovanni and Gentile Bellini's works were destroyed by fire in 1577. But even if none of their works remained, we would be able to measure their importance by the gigantic accomplishments of two of their students: Giorgione (1478?–1510) and Titian (1477?–1576). It was these masters who made a High Renaissance in Venice. And it was Titian's pupil Tintoretto (1518–94) who stepped beyond the Renaissance and helped make way for 98 another style, another trend, another age.

Giorgione

"Everybody makes his own Giorgione."

So wrote an Italian historian less than one hundred years ago. There has been so much disagreement about the artist's life that writers have been able to choose whatever details suit their stories. In various books the reader can find Giorgione first depicted as a peasant's son and elsewhere as the illegitimate child of wealthy parents who supported him in comfort. Here we read that he was extremely productive, there that he painted just a few pictures. In one account his fame spread throughout Italy; in another his influence was confined to Venice. Even Vasari, who was seldom at a loss for material (real or invented) about his subjects, could write no more than two pages about Giorgione.

His name was an Italian variation of George: Zorzo, Zorzi, or Giorgio. A big, tough man, he came to be called Zorzon (Big George) da Castelfranco (of Castelfranco, a village in Venetia). The name Giorgione, a more formal version of "Big George," was not used until about sixty years after his death.

The information offered here is based on the writing of Vasari. Giorgione was born in 1478, or perhaps a year earlier. Raised in Venice, he was as big in character and intelligence as he was in body. He was well mannered and especially gallant to the ladies, among whom he was extremely popular. His earliest association with the rich of Venice was not as an artist but as a musician. Fond of lute music, he accompanied it with his beautiful singing voice at important Venetian music festivals. But he chose painting as a career, studied with the Bellini, and soon surpassed his masters in the depiction of the most beautiful subjects.

Giorgione was less a storyteller, less bound to Florentine-Roman tradition than were the Bellini. His position in Venetian painting was much like Masaccio's in Florence: he learned from the work that preceded him, broke from prevailing traditions, and founded a new school of painting. He cared less about scientific realism and more about grandeur and expressiveness. Above all, he was concerned with organization: each element in his pictures contributes to an over-all rhythm and harmony and motion. Even his outlines are dotted and disconnected, his brushstrokes "tremble" in order to impart a total effect of unity and movement. Color, vibrant and alive, was used more brilliantly than it ever had been before; and it paved the way for Titian, who made color even more brilliant.

The Three Philosophers (see page 105), an oil painting of 1507, was quite a departure from conventional Italian art. Although the picture depicts only three figures standing and sitting on a rock in a small forest clearing, the panorama of Venetian painting is retained. But the vastness of the scene is accomplished through depth, not width. One-third of the canvas is dark; the philosophers are located on the opposite third. In the middle, however, a small space between the trees reveals a landscape so well detailed, so clearly lighted, so very deep that the viewer feels the great size of the countryside and the picturesque beauty of the vast Alpine foothills. This Giorgione captured in a picture of much greater simplicity than the Bellini would have painted. His philosophers are busy thinking important thoughts, yet one rests and glances through a small window to see the beauty of nature. He will, we gather, return to the conversation in- spired.

Giorgione cared deeply about beauty for its own sake. His people are healthy and lovely. Unlike Raphael, however, he cared very little about telling a story. What his figures do is less interesting than where they do it. The philosophers may be talking, but what they are saying is unimportant. The viewer may decide that because the men have chosen so lovely a spot for their conversation, their wisdom will be stimulated. In Giorgione's *Pastoral Symphony* of 1509 (see page 106), the little concert is so gracefully described that we can't help but sense the pleasures that must have been stirred by the music.

Giorgione much preferred classical or legendary subject matter to religious ones. But when he did choose (or was commissioned to execute) a religious subject, his approach remained the same. He praised nature and he used it to provide the tone and spirit of his paintings. In many ways he was the forerunner of landscape painters. He had a tremendous influence on the French in the seventeenth century. Nicolas Poussin (1594–1665) and Claude Lorrain (1600–1682) studied his work; in their own pictures they reduced the size and importance of figures and made the landscape itself more important. In the same century the Dutch removed the figures altogether, and landscape painting became a major kind of art.

Giorgione began a successful association with Titian in 1508. Two years later a plague invaded Venice, and Giorgione fell victim. He was only about thirty-two when he died, but his associate and unofficial student, Titian, carried on the master's work.

Titian

When a great person is born, no one (except Michelangelo's father) knows that he will be great, and records of his birth and childhood are not kept with exceptional care. Therefore, readers of historical biographies are familiar with the words "birthdate unknown" and "very little is known about his early life." Titian was born between 1476 and 1488. In his case, however, our uncertainty has nothing to do with a lack of records; it is the result of too many records. Titian lied about his age constantly, and the records of his time contain any number of different dates.

Titian was proud and ambitious. As an artist, he matured fairly late and did not develop an individual, original style until he was about forty years old. His pride made him want to conceal his late development, so he frequently told people he was younger than he was. At other times, when applying for a commission, he wanted to give the impression that he was a colleague, rather than a student, of Giovanni Bellini; so he added years to his age. Scholars have been looking into the matter for centuries. Today they generally agree that the artist was born in 1476 or 1477.

Apparently Titian did everything possible to make up for his slow start. Extremely industrious, he became one of the five or six most productive painters of all time. It seems also that Titian planned to live forever. He almost did. Indeed, if a plague had not swept Venice in 1576, when the master was, or was approaching one hundred, he might be painting still.

His full name was Tiziano Vecelli, and he was born to a well-to-do family in Pieve di Cadore, a village in the Alps about seventy miles north of Venice. At a very young age he went to Venice, and he seldom went back to Cadore; yet his home had impressed him deeply. Although Titian's work has come to typify sixteenth-century Venetian painting, the artist never once included the city, with its lovely architecture and glamorous canals, in his pictures. Instead, when choosing backgrounds, he reached into memory and recalled the picturesque scenery of his Alpine birthplace.

Arriving in Venice—he must have been about twelve or fourteen years old—Titian went first to the studio of a forgotten Venetian artist. Then he moved on to the workshops of the Bellini, where he learned to use oil paint in the Flemish manner. By 1508 he was working with Giorgione. The frescoes which the two men executed together no longer exist, but according to accounts of the time, it was impossible to tell which parts were Titian's and which were Giorgione's, for their styles were indistinguishable.

In 1515 Giovanni Bellini, who had been decorating the Ducal palace, became too ill to continue working, and Titian took over. A year later Giovanni died; and his title, Official Painter of the Republic of Venice, more or less automatically went to Titian, since he was working on the palace. As official painter, he had the opportunity to meet many important Venetians, among them the Duke of Ferrara, his first great patron. In the year 1518 he completed an altarpiece, *The* 103

Assumption of the Virgin (see page 112), in the Frari Church.

The Assumption marks the point at which Titian the artist reached maturity. He had learned to use oil paint with greater skill than had any other Italian. It was Titian, in fact, who revealed the many advantages that oils afforded an artist, and from Titian onward oil all but eclipsed the older media.

Titian prepared his canvas with a flat coat of tempera and began applying paint in thin, transparent glazes. Thus, all of his colors were the results of layer upon layer of varied hues. Color was more important to him than it had been to any artist before him: this is why his charcoal and ink sketches are not nearly so highly prized as his paintings. There are very few outlines; forms blend into warm and deep shadows, and his canvases are bathed in a soft luster that makes all his colors sparkle like jewels.

Although his religious pictures were done with tenderness and understanding, Titian was not a very devout man. Perhaps this lack of involvement was reflected in his paintings, which were not entirely well received. His paintings of subjects from classical mythology, however, were more widely applauded. Painted with clarity and a sense of humor, such pictures as *Bacchus and Ariadne* (see page 111) illustrate the artist's fondness for legendary subjects. Titian was an active, lustful man with a great appreciation for the beauty of the female body. He used his mythological pictures to express his passion, and he frankly hoped to stir passionate feelings in the people who looked at his paintings. Later, he would be one of the first artists to depict the nude female form. Since Titian, the female nude has been a favorite subject for artists.

Giorgione. *Three Philosophers.*

Detail from Giorgione's *Three Philosophers*

Giorgione. *Pastoral Symphony.*   *Louvre, Paris*

above: Detail of Raphael's *Madonna del Cardel-lino* represents the academic school of paintings; *below:* detail of Titian's *Lavinia* (reproduction, p. 111) represents the painterly school.

Gentile Bellini. *Procession of the Holy Cross.*

109

Titian.
Portrait of a Man.

The National Gallery, London

Uffizi Gallery, Florence

Giovanni Bellini.
Sacred Allegory.

Titian. *Bacchus and Ariadne.*

The National Gallery, London

Titian. *Lavinia.*

Gemaldegalerie State Museum, Berlin

But it was with the portrait that Titian earned his earliest great success. The great portrait traditionally has been a picture that captures the character of the subject but is before all else a good painting. The same rules for judging any picture apply to a portrait: the quality of line and color is no less important, and the portrait must be well composed. A good likeness is not enough. The picture must also express the artist's viewpoint. Titian approached a portrait not only with great artistic sense but with a fine business sense as well.

Titian was a terrific businessman. He had a publicity agent, regarded his patrons as customers, and was always on the lookout for new ones. His popularity as a portraitist was great, for he painted his subjects as they pictured themselves. He was a flatterer—there can be no doubt about that—but his wasn't the kind of flattery that necessarily made his subjects better looking than they really were. Guided by his own notions of how a Venetian nobleman should look, he made his subject fit the idea—not the other way around. Thus the patron would see in the portrait a noble, superior person of great strength and character who was, in fact, himself. In other words, Titian simply used the sitter's features to express his own point of view, and since he regarded the aristocrats as the superior beings of the earth, his customers went home happy.

He was also every inch a painter. Before he released a portrait, Titian sent the sitter away and went to work on the painting, adding color here, changing lines there, unifying the different parts of the canvas. Then he would turn it to the wall and leave it there for several weeks. When he re- 113

opposite: Titian. *Assumption of the Virgin.*

S. M. Gloriosa dei Frari, Venice

turned to his work his eye was extremely critical, and he would go at it again with a fresh approach. However true it may have been that Titian was conceited and self-centered, we must give him credit for his greatest quality as an artist: he had the ability to detach himself from his own work, to look at it as dispassionately as the sternest of critics, to be honest with himself and, if necessary, very hard on himself. He was very much concerned with making his patrons happy, but he demanded of himself that he produce truly flawless works of art.

In a moment of weakness in 1525, Titian married a barber's daughter named Cecelia. The artist had been seeing her for a number of years before their marriage, but he regarded her as low and stupid and never took her to important social functions. Yet he was sometimes capable of brief periods of great affection for her, and it was during one such period that he agreed to marry her. Thereafter he paid almost no attention to her, and when she died in 1530 he did not grieve but thought of himself as freed from a union he never should have formed. He was, however, devoted to his two sons, one of whom became his student, and to his daughter, Lavinia. He loved her very much, and she was one of his favorite subjects for portraiture (see page 111).

Titian made his only visit to Rome in 1545. Pope Paul III welcomed him, he was made a citizen of Rome, and everyone of importance, including Michelangelo, called on him to pay his respects. Vasari himself was assigned as his guide. He painted one picture in Rome, *Danae,* which Michelangelo and Vasari criticized: the quality of line and form, they said, had been sacrificed to color. This criticism was to be expected, for central Italian painters traditionally were less concerned with color than were the Venetians and more interested in lines, shapes, and composition. Actually, their remarks were directed more at Venetian painting in general than at Titian in particular. Titian left Rome and went to Austria to see Emperor Charles V. He became court painter to Charles, and the Hapsburgs became his principal patrons.

He was growing old, but in his personal affairs Titian seemed to grow younger with the years. He lived a ribald and active life, heavily influenced and scheduled by his publicity agent, Pietro Aretino. A writer and talentless artist, Aretino was well known as a spy, blackmailer, and embezzler, but he was absolutely devoted to Titian. At every Venetian party and pageant, the two old men would appear with great commotion and two or three very young women hanging from each arm. (How differently do peoples react from excess! The aging Titian was twice Raphael's age at peak, twice as active, three times more corrupt; all that this did for Titian was to make him more youthful.)

His approach to his work remained youthful, too. His style seemed to become more spontaneous, more dramatic, and bolder. He cared less about small details and more about the events he was depicting. Instead of becoming a petty old man, he behaved as though only big issues in a painting were important. It is interesting to note that Titian's technique, which is to this day given as an example to art students, is best exemplified in his later work.

Many painters, especially those just learning their craft, begin a picture with great enthusiasm. They view their canvas as a whole and attack it boldly with broad brushstrokes and loose drawing. But as the picture takes shape, the artist tends to concentrate on certain areas and then specific details. He begins with a number twelve brush and ends with a double zero; he starts out with big sweeps of his whole arm and finishes with little movements of the fingers, holding his brush as though it were a pencil. Most great artists, on the other hand, begin and end with the same boldness. In Titian's work this is obvious. The master used big brushes almost exclusively. He painted all over the canvas, never allowing himself to get involved with it part by part. It is said that when he was old and too easily tired to stand continuously while painting, Titian would tie his brushes to long bamboo poles, which he would manipulate from a chair placed across the studio. Then he would push his chair close to the canvas, lean on the back of it with one hand and work the paint with the fingers of the other. He used his whole arm and twists of the wrist to paint, and his final gesture was as big and bold as his first. No wonder that his later work was so admired by the French impressionists of the nineteenth century, who were the forerunners of the modern age in painting.

Titian helped to change the nature of his profession. His merchant-customer relationship led to the end of the patronage system and to the beginning of the dealership system. He made oil paint the principal medium of his art, and he set the painterly technique on its way. But before all else he was the master craftsman of the Renaissance. When he died, on August 27, 1576, the Italian Renaissance in painting was over.

Tintoretto

Although Tintoretto cannot properly be called a Renaissance painter, his relationship to the age was very close. The styles of the period didn't just end; they became other styles. It was Tintoretto who summed up the innovations of the Italian Renaissance—every characteristic we have discussed can be found in his work—but he did more. He added all that he had learned to one great recipe and put the mixture up to cook. If it wasn't quite right, he poured it out and started over, changing proportions and adding his own seasoning. His basic ingredients remained those of the Renaissance, but the final result was a style called mannerism.

Like Giotto, who came along just in time to bridge the Middle Ages and the Renaissance, Tintoretto was born at a good time in the right place. The grandeur of the age existed before his eyes, but times were changing and artists were challenged to seek new ways of painting.

His name was Jacopo Robusti, and his life began in Venice in the autumn of 1518. Because his father was a *tintore,* a dyer of silks, the boy was nicknamed Tintoretto, "little dyer." At about fourteen he was apprenticed to Titian, but according to accounts of the time, he was soon expelled from the studio. Some stories say that he was too independent and refused to follow Titian's instructions. Others say that the other students were so jealous of Tintoretto's ability that work was disrupted, giving the master no choice but to order the young artist to leave. In any case, Tintoretto went on to other teachers, although who they were is uncertain.

An extremely hard worker, Tintoretto set his goals high. 117

It is said that in his studio he tacked up a large sign which read, *The drawing of Michelangelo, the color of Titian*. To combine these was his goal, but he constantly strove for something new. He painted the same subjects over and over again. The Last Supper, you will recall, had been a favorite subject for artists until Leonardo painted his version. Thereafter artists were reluctant to use it because they knew theirs would be compared with Leonardo's *Last Supper*. But Tintoretto took on the challenge. He depicted the subject no less than a dozen times, each time attempting a different approach (see pages 130, 131). Whether any of his was equal to Leonardo's is a matter of varying opinions, but it is generally agreed that Tintoretto was the only artist after Leonardo whose *Last Supper* brought originality to the theme.

Although he was made a member of the master painters' guild in 1539, Tintoretto did not achieve widespread recognition until 1548, when his *Miracle of St. Mark* (see page 129) was completed. Most viewers admired the picture, but more than a few did not. They thought that the artist had placed too little emphasis on the subject and too much on technique. But this indeed was the direction that Tintoretto had chosen to take. Throughout his life he sought new ways to tell old stories.

Tintoretto was a fine craftsman, yet many artists criticized his application of technique. He was more religious than most Venetians, yet the Church was not always fond of his work. Into scenes depicting solemn religious moments he might paint a commonplace, frivolous incident: even in many of his Last Suppers not everyone is paying attention. He was very much a modernist and felt that religion, like painting, could use some modernizing.

For a Venetian, Tintoretto lived a somewhat modest life. He had few friends and was not much of a talker. What excesses he did have he was able to enjoy privately. He had a long marriage and eight children, three of whom—including a daughter—were among his many assistants. Before all else he was a painter, and though he was an intelligent person, he was interested by very little other than his work. When he was especially excited by a commission or a project he had made for himself, he devoted all his time to it and let his assistants handle everything else. In the last twenty years of his life he began to influence many younger painters; and after his death on May 31, 1594, his effect on the development of painting was, for a while, greater than that of any other Venetian.

Tintoretto was by no means the only mannerist, nor did he invent the style called mannerism. He was, however, one of the few artists whose work was representative of the style to the exclusion of other styles. In contrast, Michelangelo was a Renaissance artist whose last paintings became mannerist; the painter called Caravaggio (Michelangelo Merisi, 1573–1610) began as a mannerist and developed into a baroque stylist.

The style is not easy to describe. In the first place, the word *mannerism* itself has rather vague meaning. Simply stated, it refers to a kind of painting in which technique—or manner of painting—is stressed above other considerations. The mannerists exaggerated, distorted, elongated, and foreshortened in order to capture the drama of a scene. Because all artists use these methods to some degree, deciding who is and who is not a mannerist is a matter of personal judgment. To some scholars any painter who employs technique as an end in itself, valued for its own sake, is a mannerist. To others mannerism refers only to the style of painting that bridged the Renaissance and the baroque. Moreover, there is a difference between mannerist painters and the Mannerist School. The latter was a group of artists who considered themselves successors to Tintoretto and Caravaggio, whose "manner" of painting was imitated.

The great innovations of the Renaissance were behind Tintoretto. He made thorough studies of the works of the Italian masters. He saw how they had employed the effects of light, and he attempted to go a step further. After making small, simple figures of clay, he placed them in a box into which he had cut one window. Then he lighted a candle outside the window and moved it about, carefully noting the changing effects of the light on the figures. He saw how the masters had learned and used anatomy, and he experimented and discovered how much he could exaggerate the body without making it look unreasonable. He studied the rules of perspective, from which he would depart in order to increase the appearance of depth. He even used perspective to render the human body. He would try anything—distort any line, enrich any color, depict any subject from the most unexpected angle—to make his pictures more dramatic.

Tintoretto's mannerism led to the baroque style of the seventeenth century. There are a number of elements in his work that the later artists seized: in any Tintoretto paintings, the principal subjects are frozen in descriptive, almost theatrical poses. They are highlighted by a dramatic kind of lighting—not unlike a spotlight on a partially darkened stage. The sense of depth is very great and makes the viewer search the subtly lighted shadows for other people and details. Furniture, jewels, fabrics, and architectural decorations are modeled quite beautifully and gently highlighted. Frequently, half-hidden by shadows, comrades drink or a boy and girl converse. This observation of the commonplace in painting is called *genre* and was a major baroque subject for such masters as Hals and Rembrandt.

When Tintoretto's mannerism was beginning to attract attention, his greatness was a subject of debate in Venice. No one denied that his ability to render the human figure was comparable only to Michelangelo's, but his technique was often thought too showy, too dependent on tricks. Aretino, Titian's publicity agent, was a man who liked to be right and who liked to prove how good his judgment was. When he first saw Tintoretto's work, he gave it his approval. Then, as he heard the debate, he decided that in the end, Tintoretto would probably not achieve great success; so he withdrew his endorsement and became the artist's most bitter critic. Everywhere he went, Aretino would make jokes about Tintoretto and deride his work. After about a year of this— a year in which Tintoretto had managed to survive the critical storm and receive more commissions—the artist decided to do something about Aretino's insults. He offered to paint the troublemaker's portrait, and, never one to turn down anything free, Aretino agreed. As he took his position on the model-stand he struck a pose and saw Tintoretto standing at the easel with a pistol. He asked what the gun was for. "It is my measuring stick," Tintoretto explained. "You, Aretino, are three pistols high." Never again did the master hear of criticism from the mouth of Aretino.

THE
OTHER RENAISSANCE

There were, in a manner of speaking, two Renaissances.

One was a very specific period in history. Based on a re-vival of classicism, it began in the fourteenth century, took hold in the fifteenth, and did not outlive the sixteenth. Italy was its one and only home. When the heart of Western civ-ilization moved northward, first to France and then to Great Britain, the Italian Renaissance ended.

The other Renaissance was more an attitude than an age. It was based on the spirit of humanism, with its stress on in-dividual achievement. Stimulating exploration and experi-ment in science, politics, religion, and the arts, it spread throughout Europe. From its Italian origin it expanded and expanded until it had become woven into the fabric of Western life. Then, at a moment too vague to pinpoint, it stopped being the Renaissance and became the modern world.

Home of the last great ancient empire, Italy was the only country in the Roman Catholic world capable of giving new life to classicism. During the Classical Age, most of Europe was inhabited by tribes of wanderers and barbarians. Therefore, it was not possible for Germany or the Netherlands to have a true Renaissance; for in the countries north of the Alps, there was no classical heritage to be reborn.

Yet it is of little importance that the Italian word *renaissance* means rebirth. What is important is that the spirit of intellectual curiosity that the Italian Renaissance characterized had a tremendous effect on all of Europe. The so-called Northern Renaissance may not have been a real rebirth, but it did exist.

Within a century or two after the Italian Renaissance had begun, its spirit inspired radical changes in the patterns of European life. The Church, for example, had been almost above criticism in the Middle Ages. The Renaissance loosened the Vatican's grip. With the Protestant Reformation in the sixteenth century, Christianity divided; and by the 1600s there were several new Christian faiths, some more liberal and some much stricter than Catholicism. Geographical exploration—an outgrowth of the Renaissance spirit—influenced the ambitions of Europe. Some say that Christopher Columbus's having to leave home to find support for his trip was an indication that the Italian predominance was on the decline. In any case, exploration and discovery became the goals of the day.

The pattern in art was the same. As mannerism led to 123

the style called baroque, Italy continued to produce great artists. But the number was smaller, and the struggle for artistic supremacy centered on Spain and France, Flanders and Holland.

The struggle began just before 1500. With the eyes of Europe fixed on Italy, kings began to realize that great art was integral to the building of great nations. Italians were invited abroad; and in return, rulers sent their own artists to study in Italy. All over Europe painters and sculptors began to experience the same heroic importance that Italians had been enjoying for some time. But to the credit of the foreign artists, Italian art remained an influence and a guide, not a model to be copied.

The Flemish were rightfully proud of their own traditions. What they learned from the Italians they applied to their very personal, very Flemish techniques.

The Germans had an entirely different temperament from the Italians. Proud and orderly, very much concerned with mystery and death, the Germans were more strongly influenced by the Gothic Age than were any other Europeans. Humanism never appealed to their artists, but the Renaissance emphasis on scholarship and skill did.

In its struggle to resist the tides of secularism and reform, Spain became the most rigidly Catholic country in Europe. It shared the spreading interest in art, scholarship, and exploration; but it adapted Renaissance ideas to its own needs. From the painting of a picture to the colonization of America, all things were devoted to the glorification of "God and country."

124 On the other extreme was France, whose artists most de-

liberately tried to imitate the art of the Italian Renaissance. The French envied and admired the Italians. However childish their attempts at making themselves the successors of the Italians may have been, the French did finally develop a unique kind of art. By the seventeenth century, France had become the center of European artistic activity; and Paris remained the world's art capital for three hundred years.

Finally, England, under King Henry VIII, reached out for its own Renaissance. Despite their gigantic accomplishments in politics, literature, drama, and war, the English suffered from a lack of skilled native-born artists. Realizing this, Henry imported as many foreign artists as would come. Although a superb period of English Renaissance architecture resulted, the achievements of British painters were more modest. An excellent school of portrait painting developed, but this was peculiar to the country and only slightly related to the Renaissance. (What England lacked in painting, it should be added, was more than made up for by the magnificence of its literature.)

The best non-Italians who are known as Renaissance painters were those who applied Italian influences to their own traditions. Two such artists were Albrecht Dürer (1471–1528), a German (see page 134), and Pieter Brueghel the Elder (1525?–69), a Fleming (see pages 133, 134). Another, known as El Greco (1541–1614), typified the international effects of the Renaissance (see pages 135, 136).

Above all others it is Dürer who is credited with introducing the Renaissance to northern Europe. When he was born, artists in Germany were regarded as little more than craftsmen. By the time of his death, artists were honored 125 and respected. Dürer himself was admired for his scholarship as well as for his artistic talents.

тhe other
кenaissance

Dürer was born in Nuremberg, and until he was fifteen, he worked with his father, a modestly prosperous goldsmith. Then he worked in a local studio where woodcut illustrations were prepared for printed books. The young artist learned his trade well. He remained a much greater printmaker than painter; indeed, he was probably the greatest maker of woodcut prints in the history of art.

In 1494 Dürer and his wife, Agnes, went to Venice, where he learned of the Italian Renaissance firsthand. After his second trip, in 1505, his work began to show the Italian influence. Combining the classical harmony of Italian painting with the Gothic qualities of his native German style, Dürer captured the interest of other northern artists, who sought his consultation and advice. He told his students about the great ideas of the time; for he had studied mathematics, geometry, Latin, and literature in Italy. Among his friends were some of Europe's most powerful men: Martin Luther, Giovanni Bellini, and the Emperor Maximilian I, ruler of the Holy Roman Empire. The Emperor, in fact, placed Dürer in a position to have the greatest possible influence. The master was made court painter and was given a pension for life.

Thus did the Renaissance come to Germany. Classical subject matter, emphasis on anatomy and perspective, and a sense of orderliness affected German painting. Yet Dürer and his followers retained much that was characteristic of German art. Unlike the Italians, who preferred to stress the whole form, the Germans traditionally concentrated on the power and relationships of individual lines. Mystery and death hover over their pictures, which are linear and intricately detailed.

Dürer's position in the North was comparable only with Michelangelo's in Italy. He was celebrated in the smallest towns, and he was known to everyone, from peasant to Emperor. He was a hero in the truest Renaissance sense.

Flanders, which is now Belgium and the Burgundy province of France, was united with the Netherlands under the Dukes of Burgundy throughout the fifteenth and sixteenth centuries. In 1609, however, the Protestant north became the Dutch Republic, while Flanders remained Catholic.

The Flemish were the only people in Europe who were confident that their own art was the match for Italy's. Perhaps because of this confidence, the Flemish had a fine relationship with Italy.

In the 1400s the Low Countries enjoyed an artistic era as unique as the one in Florence. Flemish artists were far more interested in capturing absolute realism than were the Italians. Their concern with detail can be compared to the German attitude; but they had a much more down-to-earth, more civilized approach. In the sixteenth century this approach bloomed into an interest in all things earthly.

Most expressive of sixteenth-century Flemish art was the work of the Elder Brueghel. He spent most of his life in Antwerp, married, and had two sons who were also fine painters. Very little else is known about his personal life.

Brueghel was among the first landscape painters who ever lived. From his landscapes he became fairly well known and was made a member of the guild of master painters. 127

Midway in his career he became interested in the human figure. In many of his brightly colored pictures, patterns are created by crowds of people; but these were not the gods or religious figures of Italian painting. They were farmers at work in the fields and village folk dancing and feasting at festivals. The figures are arranged in groups that give great movement and rhythmic quality to the scenes. Using peasants in his religious paintings, Brueghel illustrated Bible stories that tell of the sins and follies of mankind. In his intertwining of scenery and event, Brueghel is firmly in the Flemish realist tradition; but his work also reaches back to the master Giotto.

Brueghel's sons and grandsons continued the Flemish tradition, which, combined with the mannerism of Italy, led to the international baroque style of the seventeenth century.

There were no planes, no telephones, no vehicles that traveled at great speed; but in the sixteenth century the world was getting smaller. Everywhere in Europe the transition from the Middle Ages to modern times was complete. The unity—bloody though it may have been—that the Church had brought to the continent was gone. Countries bound by language were formed to compete with other countries. Though the world was more closely integrated than it had been, peoples understood each other less. Styles of art crossed tightly guarded and jealously defended borders that were often closed to human beings. Neighbors, perhaps, could be trusted, but foreigners, never.

Kyriakos Theotokopoulos, known as El Greco (the Greek), lived the life of a foreigner. Born on the island of Crete, which had once been Greek, he was not a Greek citi-

Tintoretto. *Miracle of St. Mark.*   *Academy Gallery, Venice*

Tintoretto. *The Last Supper.*

San Giorgio Maggiore, Venice

Tintoretto. *The Last Supper.*

San Marcuola, Venice

Representative European Renaissance Painters

Hans Holbein the Younger.
Portrait of Henry VIII.

National Gallery, Rome

Clouet. *Portrait of Francis I.*

Louvre, Paris

Pieter Brueghel the Elder. *The Wedding Dance.* *Detroit Institute of Arts*

El Greco. *View of Toledo.*   Metropolitan Museum of Art, New York

opposite: Dürer. *Melancholy* (see also detail).

   Fogg Museum of Art, Harvard University

opposite: Pieter Brueghel the Elder. *The Hired Shepherd.*

   Johnson Collection, Philadelphia Museum of Art

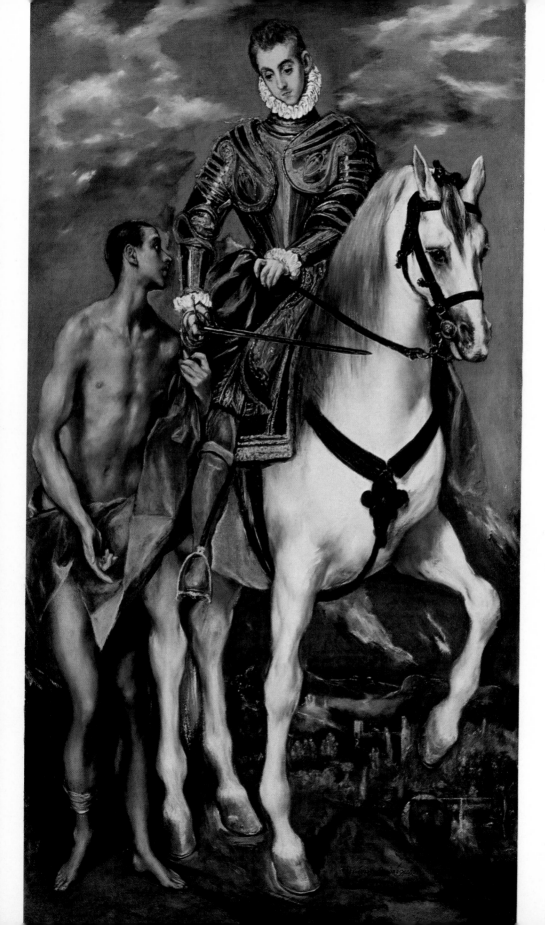

zen; for the island was occupied by the Venetians. The Venetian conquerors had made themselves comfortable and treated the conquered natives as foreigners.

When Crete had been Greek it was part of the Eastern Christian world. Therefore, El Greco grew up surrounded by remains of Byzantine art. This influence was very important to the artist, and the Eastern touch never left his work.

In his early twenties El Greco left the island and went to Venice. His talent was recognized by Titian, who became his teacher. But El Greco did not make good in Venice. Regarded as a strange, unpredictable, and religious foreigner, he was not made to feel especially welcome. He left and went to Rome.

Before long El Greco had impressed the Romans—in the worst possible way. Michelangelo had just finished *The Last Judgment*. Encouraged by several of his advisors, the Pope had asked the artist to clothe some of the nude figures in the mural. Michelangelo had refused, and a great controversy raged in Rome. El Greco, standing in the Sistine Chapel, said he didn't care whether or not the figures were covered but volunteered to settle the argument. He proposed that the mural should be destroyed and that he would paint another just as good. For anyone to insult the heroic Michelangelo in those days was a dangerous business; for a foreigner to do so was not to be tolerated. Realizing that he would never again find work in Rome, El Greco quietly departed.

He went to Spain and settled in the city of Toledo (see page 135). No one could pronounce his name, and it was there that he came to be called El Greco. Never a favorite of the Madrid court, he did earn commissions from the churchmen around Toledo, where he remained until his death.   137

opposite: El Greco. *St. Martin and the Beggar.*

National Gallery, Washington, D. C.

The origins of El Greco's style of painting were truly international. Byzantine, Greek classical, and Italian Renaissance art all affected his work. But it was the Spanish influence that completed the making of El Greco the painter. Then as now, the proud and passionate Spanish people inspired widely varied impressions in the minds of foreigners. El Greco was one who believed the Spanish to be the most deeply feeling people in the West. He embraced the spirit of Spain and tried to express the Spanish soul in his work.

El Greco would try anything to illustrate emotions, sacrifice any detail in order to portray passion. Be it a person at night, the sky at dusk, a tree swaying in a storm, or a windblown set of draperies, everything in an El Greco picture has life of its own. The artist thought that a feeling of life in art could be captured less by anatomy than by the careful depiction of movement. Thus he distorted the human figure in order to describe the way it moved. Applying paint thickly and thinly, he emphasized his brushstrokes instead of trying to hide them. The light with which he bathed his subjects is sometimes threatening and mysterious, at other times soft and heavenly.

El Greco was the supreme mannerist; for the effects of his pictures come from his technique. The boldness of his brushstroke, the energy of his approach, the freedom with which he applied paint, and the harshness of his earthy colors are perfect complements to the passionate subjects he chose. Although he was not a Spaniard, he made a style of art ideally suited to the Spanish temperament. And after the death of El Greco, Spain began making important contributions to the development of international styles.

The Italian Renaissance was the body in which a new spirit was born. When the Italian Renaissance died, the spirit survived. The Italians had brought to art and to all phases of life the idea that the individual was responsible for his own acts and for the improvement of his world. By the time Italy's Renaissance ended, this idea had been embedded in Western thought.

Explore, the founders of the Renaissance had said. Men explored, and they found the New World. Fail if you must but experiment. Men experimented, and their scientific discoveries led to the Industrial Revolution that changed the patterns of their lives. Think: take nothing for granted, and let reason guide your destiny. Men thought, and their reasoning filled them with a desire for liberty and justice. So, inspired by the Renaissance spirit and convinced by the results of their individual accomplishments, men together, shaped a modern world. They created new governments to ensure their human rights. Their participation in the industrial age they had fashioned made them prosperous. They made discoveries in science that would help them live longer and in better health. Having explored this earth to its farthest acres, they turned to the exploration of heavens and seas. And, as always, they expressed their views about man and his world through their art.

No longer located in any such picturesque setting as the Medici garden, the center of scientific achievement has shifted across an ocean. Within the great twentieth-century towers of glass, steel, and concrete that rise from mechanical streets to pierce the American sky, ideas intertwine and shape the course of civilization. Men and nations continue to explore, to experiment, and to reason.

The Renaissance seems long passed, an age gone forever. But the sky and the depths of the sea, medicine and invention, books and paintings are still at the center of man's curiosity. These great subjects that challenge the modern mind are the very same ones that fascinated Leonardo da Vinci, the man of the Renaissance.

READING AND LOOKING

Although most Renaissance art remains in or near the places where it was created, some splendid works have been relocated. The National Gallery in London owns one of the finest collections of Renaissance paintings outside continental Europe. In the United States most large municipal museums contain something representative of the period; especially important are the collections in Boston's Gardner Museum, New York's Frick Collection, and the city museums in Boston, Detroit, and Philadelphia. But the largest and most significant Renaissance collections in America hang in the Art Institute, Chicago, the Metropolitan Museum of Art, New York, and the National Gallery of Art, Washington, D.C. Traveling exhibitions reach many small museums nowadays. For this reason—and a hundred others— 141

it would be to your advantage to put your name on the
mailing list of the museums in your area. (Citizens of the
United States, no matter where they live, are entitled to receive the informative bulletins of the National Gallery of
Art free of charge—an unusual bargain.)

Anyone who wants to learn more about the artists of the
Renaissance should have no trouble finding fascinating
books in the art section of the public library. One word of
advice: keep in mind the difference between a biography
and a fiction-biography. While the historian-writer is concerned with describing the events in his subject's life in order
that the reader might better understand the artist's work,
the novelist's primary aim is to create a work of art. There
is nothing wrong about this: like any artist, the writer of
fiction owns what we call poetic license—a license to change
the facts as much as he has to to make his book better. If
you must read fiction-biographies, remember that the story
may be very different from the real circumstances of the
artist's life. But a better idea is to find a non-fiction biography first. The truth may be more fun anyway.

The books named below are by no means the only good
ones available on the subject of Renaissance painting, nor
are they necessarily the best. They have been listed here
simply because they are interesting, clearly written, and ex-
pand on the material covered in this book.

Berenson, Bernard, *Italian Painters of the Renaissance*.
Cleveland: World, 1957. (Paperback)
Brooks, Polly S. and Walworth, Nancy Z. *The World
Awakes*. Philadelphia: Lippincott, 1962.

Murray, Peter. *Art of the Renaissance*. New York: Praeger, 1963.

Craven, Thomas. *The Rainbow Book of Art*. Cleveland: World, 1956.

Ketchum, Richard M., ed. *The Horizon Book of the Renaissance*. New York: American Heritage and Doubleday, 1961.

Battisti, Eugenio. *Giotto*. New York and Cleveland: Skira and World, 1960.

Palma, Viardo, ed. *Masaccio*. New York: Abrams, 1959. (Paperback)

Williams, Jay, and Lowry, B. *Leonardo da Vinci*. New York: American Heritage and Harper & Row, 1965.

Alexander, Sidney. *Michelangelo the Florentine*. New York: Random House, 1957.

Symonds, John A. *The Life of Michelangelo*. New York: Random House, 1936.

Coletti, Luigi, ed. *All the Paintings of Giorgione*. New York: Hawthorn, 1962.

Valsecchi, Marco, ed. *Titian*. New York: Abrams, 1963. (Paperback)